COMPREHENSION INTERVENTION

Small-Group Lessons for The Comprehension Toolkit

Stephanie Harvey
Anne Goudvis
Judy Wallis

*first*hand

HEINEMANN

DEDICATED TO TEACHERS

DEDICATED TO TEACHERS

*first*hand
An imprint of Heinemann
361 Hanover Street
Portsmouth, NH 03801-3912
firsthand.heinemann.com

Offices and agents throughout the world

Cataloguing-in-Publication data for this book is available from
the Library of Congress.

ISBN-10: 0-325-03148-7
ISBN-13: 978-0-325-03148-4

Design and production: Eclipse Publishing Services
Cover photograph: David Stirling

Printed in the United States of America

14   13   12   11   10   VP   1   2   3   4   5   6

Contents

The small-group sessions in *Comprehension Intervention* reinforce the original lessons in *The Comprehension Toolkit*. The following chart correlates the original Toolkit lesson with its corresponding intervention session(s) and shows the page on which you will find the small-group session.

MONITOR COMPREHENSION

ACTIVATE AND CONNECT

ASK QUESTIONS

INFER MEANING

DETERMINE IMPORTANCE

SUMMARIZE AND SYNTHESIZE

Comprehension Intervention User's Guide

WELCOME TO COMPREHENSION INTERVENTION, a resource of small-group lessons for *The Comprehension Toolkits. The Comprehension Toolkit* and *The Primary Comprehension Toolkit* focus on practices that feature explicit, robust, in-depth comprehension instruction. Successful Toolkit instruction leads to students reading engaging texts at their level, thinking deeply about them, interacting with others, and acquiring knowledge. The Toolkit is founded on several major principles of reading, learning, and achievement. Research (adapted from Allington 2009) indicates that to become proficient readers, students must:

- spend large amounts of time reading and thinking in text they can and want to read;
- have extensive opportunities to respond to their reading through talking, writing, and drawing;
- view reading as a meaningful activity that is personally fulfilling;
- focus on big ideas, issues, and concepts across disciplines; and
- receive explicit instruction in using strategies as tools for decoding and comprehension.

The comprehension lessons in the Toolkits are primarily launch lessons that are designed to be used with the whole class to kick-start kids into wide and effective reading. In fact, they are more than just whole-group lessons. They model practices we teach again and again with a variety of texts, in different contexts, and for many different purposes. We teach these lessons in science, social studies, for research and inquiry projects, in small groups and with individuals. Comprehension instruction in the Toolkits lays a foundation of thinking so that students internalize ways to comprehend what they read and apply strategies in their own independent reading and learning. The whole point of Toolkit comprehension strategy instruction is to move kids toward independence. We view *Comprehension Intervention* as a bridge to that reading independence.

We created *Comprehension Intervention* as a resource to provide additional support to kids who need more time and more explicit instruction to integrate comprehension strategies and use them as tools for learning and understanding. One might ask, why an intervention resource that focuses exclusively on comprehension instruction? The short answer is that there are many programs out there for small-group intervention that stress decoding, fluency, and other aspects of reading, but there are few, if any, that focus intensively on comprehension.

The long answer begins with the conclusions of the final report on Reading First (Gamse, Jacob, Horst, Boulay, and Unlu 2008): "Reading First did not produce a statistically significant impact on student reading comprehension." All that time, money, and effort, and kids apparently didn't get better at what really matters in reading, constructing meaning. So the small-group sessions in *Comprehension Intervention* provide authentic comprehension instruction that engages kids and teaches them to think actively as they read. Now we don't for a minute believe that kids don't need to be taught to decode the words, but surface-structure resources abound. *Comprehension Intervention* fills a void and provides a reading resource that teaches kids to think, to understand, and to use strategies as tools for learning. That, to our way of thinking, is what comprehension is all about.

FROM WHOLE GROUP TO SMALL GROUP

Of late, whole-group instruction has gotten a bad rap. And we understand why. Endless recitation sessions, reams of fill-in-the-blank worksheets, and kids reading the text out loud in unison often characterize whole-group work. And this isn't hyperbole. According to Pianta, Belsky, Houts, and Morrison (2007), students spend about 92% of the school day in their seats listening to the teacher or doing individual seatwork. But whole-group instruction does not have to look like this.

In Toolkit whole-group learning, kids participate in guided discussions designed to get at significant issues, ideas, and concepts that matter. The teacher acts more as a "guide on the side" than a "sage on the stage." Kids do much of the work—interacting with one another and responding throughout the lesson by talking, writing, and drawing. Rich talk about text leads to greater understanding and long-term learning. These active conversations help students transfer their collaborative thinking into their own reading. Discussions about shared texts build a community of learners, thinkers, and communicators who ask questions, debate opinions, build and actively use knowledge, work as a team, and ultimately care about each other and their place in the world.

We emphasize whole-group instruction in *The Comprehension Toolkit* and *The Primary Comprehension Toolkit* for two main reasons. First, we want all kids to engage in the spirited discussions and interactions that characterize Toolkit instruction so they can all contribute their thoughts and ideas to whole-class conversations. Kids in need of additional support should not be pulled out during the whole-class Toolkit lessons. The shared readings in the Toolkit whole-group lessons give all kids the chance to engage, participate, and learn from each other. Secondly, in whole-group Toolkit instruction, kids get the opportunity to practice what they are learning right there in front of the teacher. They are bunched up close on the floor where all are engaged, with each other as well as with the teacher. This proximity allows the teacher to focus on their responses and to adapt instruction accordingly throughout the whole-group lesson. No more teacher doing all of the talking and kids merely staring back! All kids participate together in the active learning process. As the teacher models instruction, the kids turn and talk to one another, jot and draw thinking, and synthesize information.

During much of guided practice in the Toolkit lessons, the kids remain gathered on the floor to practice the task with a partner or on their own as the teacher touches base and confers. After time spent practicing up close with the teacher, the kids go off on their own or in pairs and continue reading and working. During this time, the teacher moves about the room meeting with the kids to support and assess how things are going. The teacher's observations guide the next instructional steps. This is when small groups come in. In short, small-group instruction does not replace whole-group instruction; it enhances it.

RESPONSIVE SMALL-GROUP INSTRUCTION

Children differ. They learn in fits and starts. What works for one may not work for another. For some, it's a matter of time. For others, it's a matter of interest. Some kids take these strategies and run with them after one whole-group Toolkit lesson. Others need additional time, guidance, and practice to internalize comprehension strategies and use them to make sense of what they read. The small-group sessions in *Comprehension Intervention* are specifically designed to support those kids. And small groups work. Pianta et al. (2007) found evidence that "opportunities to learn in small groups, to improve analytical skills, [and] to interact extensively with teachers . . . add depth to students' understanding." But small groups need to be flexible and needs-based so we can meet kids where they are and take them where they need to go.

The small-group reading and thinking strategy sessions in *Comprehension Intervention* are especially useful for kids who find comprehension problematic. We all need a quiver full of strategies to pull out when reading gets tough. Kids who have difficulty with comprehension need even more carefully scaffolded support from the teacher if they are to transfer these strategies to their own reading and thinking and turn them into tools they can use flexibly and at will. Created to follow each Toolkit lesson, the *Comprehension Intervention* small-group sessions target a specific instructional focus, concentrating on critical aspects of the Toolkit's lesson strategy to reinforce kids' understanding, step by step.

Using the language of the Toolkits in a small-group setting, *Comprehension Intervention* approaches each Toolkit strategy lesson in a new way and with new texts, showing kids that they can apply the thinking and strategy language they learned within the whole group to a wide variety of readings.

Responsive instruction is differentiation at its best. *Comprehension Intervention* lays out a framework for effective small-group instruction and builds the following best practices into differentiated instruction.

These small-group sessions provide the perfect opportunity to:

- Scaffold comprehension instruction, providing guidance to kids and instant feedback to teachers
- Zero in on comprehension strategies as tools for understanding
- Provide flexible differentiated instruction based on individual needs
- Focus on key Toolkit goals in need of reinforcement
- Reinforce the strategy language and concepts of the Toolkit lessons
- Extend the time dedicated to guided practice, giving kids opportunities to read and use strategies with text at their level and the teacher right there
- Keep sessions child-focused and fast-paced with kids doing most of the work
- Break down strategy lessons into smaller parts and teach those explicitly
- Use engaging text to promote new learning in the context of real reading
- Match texts to kids' interests and reading levels
- Observe and assess individuals' understanding of specific strategies
- Check children's understanding of a variety of genre included in the Toolkits: nonfiction, poetry, realistic and historical fiction

ASSESSING WHILE TEACHING

Our instruction must match our kids' needs. After a whole-group lesson, we assess children's reading and convene flexible small groups based on these needs. One of the reasons we meet with small groups is so we can readily and seamlessly assess kids' progress. With a small group, we can pay very close attention to exactly what our students are thinking and doing. We can easily hear them read. We can read their Post-its quickly. And we can engage in extended conversations with them—all so we can uncover their thinking as they make sense of text (or not). So when we meet in small intervention groups, it is a 24/7 assessment opportunity. Think of it as a teaching-assessing loop, where we are continuously engaged in formative assessment. By reading students' work and listening to them read and talk, we get a good idea of what to teach next and where each student needs to go.

Comprehension Intervention focuses on ongoing formative assessment while we teach comprehension. At the end of each session, an Assess and Plan section focuses attention on key performance indicators for that session and on what might be done to address them. In the Toolkits, each lesson in each strategy book has an extensive assessment section that gives examples of kids' work accompanied by our analysis. We recommend that as you take kids through the intervention sessions, you frequently refer back to the Reflect and Assess sections of the Toolkit and use the annotated work samples and our commentary as a guide for your own assessment throughout the intervention sessions. In addition, both Toolkit and *Comprehension Intervention* have tools for summative assessment at the end of each unit.

INSTRUCTIONAL SETTINGS FOR *COMPREHENSION INTERVENTION*

Philosophically, it is important that, as teachers, we get to know kids as readers and thinkers. We watch them carefully in an effort to target our instruction to their specific needs. After kids participate in the whole-group Toolkit lesson, we form small groups based on our close observation of kids' work and progress. Our intervention groups stem from what we learn about kids as we instruct them and assess their reading. Some of these intervention groups are classroom-based and led by the classroom teacher. Others occur outside of the classroom with specialists providing the instruction. The *Comprehension Intervention* sessions can be beneficial in the following instructional settings.

Guided reading groups—Sometimes we convene small, flexible, needs-based guided reading groups to reinforce or extend what we have taught in a Toolkit lesson. In a small group, we can carefully guide instruction and gradually release kids as they demonstrate increased independence. These groups may meet two or three times or more frequently, based on kids' needs, to ensure that they are internalizing the Toolkit strategies and using them in their independent reading. These guided reading groups can be taught by the classroom teacher or a specialist.

Tier 2 RTI (Response to Intervention) groups—Tier 2 support is additional, intensive, small-group instruction delivered by the teacher or a reading specialist. Experts suggest that a Tier 2 small-group intervention might span eight to twelve weeks and is considered temporary.

"Tier 2 intervention increases the intensity of instruction…by reducing the size of the group and increasing the duration and frequency of support." (Howard 2009, 71) The best and most effective Tier 2 instruction encourages kids to spend an additional 30 minutes a day reading authentic text at their level and of interest to them, with the teacher providing explicit comprehension instruction. *The Comprehension Intervention* sessions are designed to take about 30 minutes. They break down the original Toolkit instruction into smaller steps, making learning more accessible for Tier 2 students.

Tier 3 RTI groups—Tier 3 increases the instructional intensity further by decreasing the size of the group to either one-on-one or up to three students and increasing the frequency and duration of instruction to two 30-minute daily sessions. (Howard 2009, 79) The sessions in *Comprehension Intervention* are useful because they help teachers continue to break strategy instruction down into smaller steps using a variety of texts and allowing additional time for instruction and practice.

Special education—Kids who are identified for special education and have IEPs (individual education plans) in reading can also benefit from the *Comprehension Intervention* sessions. Whether the kids go to the resource room or the special ed teacher comes into the classroom, the sessions target very specific skills and strategies and build children's comprehension over time. And perhaps best of all, the Toolkit whole-group lessons are ideal for special ed inclusion because they are based on shared readings, which allow for natural differentiation. All kids can participate in the whole-group Toolkit lessons and then have their individual needs met in the small-group intervention sessions.

Other reading support groups: Title 1, after-school tutoring, summer school, and so on—The *Comprehension Intervention* sessions offer opportunities for engaging small groups in real reading and carefully scaffolded instruction in settings outside of the classroom as well as in it. Most of the reading problems that kids demonstrate are comprehension-based, so we need to teach explicitly in a variety of small groups, such as Title 1 reading groups, summer school support, and after-school tutoring.

ORGANIZING FOR *COMPREHENSION INTERVENTION*: IN-CLASS INSTRUCTION

One reason that classroom teachers often shy away from small-group instruction is the need to keep the rest of the class occupied while they concentrate on the small group. Seriously, how can we create thoughtful, independent practice for all of the other kids while we are leading a small group? That is the $64,000 question! And it's not just about keeping kids busy. When loaded up with worksheets and other busy work, kids quickly lose interest, management issues surface, and learning goes south. Active literacy means that kids need to stay busy for sure, but busy with thoughtful work, work that stimulates, challenges, and engages them. Our solution is to take the practices from the Toolkit and set up tasks where kids can read, apply Toolkit strategies, think and question, and add to their knowledge base all on their own. When you are with a small group, the other kids can:

- Interact with images, placing Post-its of their thoughts and questions on the image and talking about it with a partner
- Read text, interacting with it by jotting their thinking and drawing what they are learning
- Listen to someone read, jotting down what they learned and what they wonder, sharing that with the reader
- Watch streaming video and write and draw questions, connections, and other thoughts while watching
- Refer to anchor charts that were created during a Toolkit lesson and use them to guide a variety of responses
- Write and draw their own books, using the many nonfiction texts and images in the room as mentor texts
- Use nonfiction features in their writing and drawing to help readers better understand what they have written
- Create posters to demonstrate learning
- Research topics related to ongoing content area units
- Create group murals of topics from the content areas that the class is studying
- Respond to and illustrate their thoughts about poetry
- Extend their learning by asking questions and searching for answers
- Go online to answer questions and find information at approved sites
- Work with several others in inquiry circles or literature circles
- Read text simply for the sake of it!!
- Participate in any other interactive process that nudges kids to think, learn, and understand

ORGANIZING FOR *COMPREHENSION INTERVENTION:* OUT-OF-CLASS INSTRUCTION

Pullout groups solve the challenge of keeping the other kids busy but create another one: How do you keep intervention instruction consistent and coherent with the foundation whole-class Toolkit lesson the kids have already experienced? This is especially difficult if another teacher or a specialist is in charge of small-group reinforcement. *Comprehension Intervention* is designed to make the transition from whole class to small group as seamless as possible. The *Comprehension Intervention* objectives and instructional language match and in some cases extend the Toolkit lessons. Pullout teachers who pick up *Comprehension Intervention* sessions for the first time and are unfamiliar with the Toolkit will still be using the same terminology, the same teaching language, and the same learning prompts with which the classroom teacher introduced the original Toolkit lesson. *Comprehension Intervention* also provides an avenue for more effective communication between the regular education teacher and the pullout specialist since the intervention sessions are designed to follow up the whole-class Toolkit lesson. The conversation between teachers can focus more explicitly on instruction because kids are working on the same strategies both in and out of the classroom. In addition, the Assess and Plan section at the end of each intervention session provides specific recommendations that can be used to coordinate with other members of a student's instructional team.

GETTING STARTED WITH *COMPREHENSION INTERVENTION*

The *Comprehension Intervention* small-group sessions are designed to follow the whole-group lessons in the Toolkits. They are effective for kids who need additional support. There is a fine line, however, between convening a small group too soon and waiting too long to reteach and reinforce the lesson.

Assessing to Plan Instruction—Before deciding on and planning to engage kids in a small intervention group, we assess them to determine if they need additional scaffolded instruction and to design that instruction. To do this, we:

- Observe children's efforts and participation during the guided, collaborative, and independent practice part of the whole-class Toolkit lesson
- Read and analyze children's responses from the whole-group lesson as well as any follow-up lessons
- Listen in on their conversations as they practice collaboratively and independently
- Listen to them read and talk to them about their reading
- Confer with them individually to assess their understanding and make sure we understand the thinking behind their written and drawn responses
- Notice how effectively they use the strategies we have taught

Based on our assessment of how purposefully and effectively students use strategies to understand what they read, we convene small intervention groups for those who need more instructional time and practice to access and use reading and thinking strategies. They frequently fall into the categories mentioned earlier: flexible guided reading groups, Tier 2 or Tier 3 RTI groups, and a variety of other reading support groups, including special education.

Gathering Appropriate Texts—We have said it before: Half of our success as teachers is getting the right texts into kids' hands. The right book or article can ignite kids' interest, launching them into a lifetime of reading. Nonfiction is the most accessible genre. Stuffed with information of every type, it is a powerful way into reading. Packed with illustrations, graphs, charts, photos, maps, and so forth, nonfiction lures the kids to jump in and explore the real world.

Although each *Comprehension Intervention* session provides suggestions for texts that are appropriate for teaching the particular lesson strategy, you will want to have an arsenal of surefire texts at hand. As we gather text for small-group comprehension instruction, we make sure that we collect a variety of nonfiction text at different levels on a wide range of topics. Kids who find reading a challenge often gravitate to the topics that they are interested in, and nonfiction frequently fills the bill. We take great care to match students with text they are interested in at their reading level. When kids are reading at their own level, they devour books and effectively use strategies not only to understand but also to think beyond the text. Above all, we make sure to build in a great deal of time for kids to actually read text at their level, so they can develop as readers and become lifelong learners.

The Toolkit lessons are primarily centered on nonfiction. Kids in small intervention groups will have had exposure to the nonfiction text in the original Toolkit lessons. For the *Comprehension Intervention* sessions, we encourage you to choose text that will fire up your kids and to match it to the reading level of most of the group. Since intervention groups average from 20–30 minutes in length, the text must be short. We offer several text possibilities in each of the *Comprehension Intervention* sessions, but you also might want to consider the following sources:

- Articles from ***Keep Reading: A Source Book of Short Text*** in *The Primary Comprehension Toolkit* and articles from ***The Source Book of Short Text*** in *The Comprehension Toolkit* for grades 3–6. In addition to the lesson texts, both of these source books include lots of additional practice texts. In the grades 3–6 *Source Book*, pages 92–135 include texts on a variety of levels and a myriad of topics from magic to the Tour de France. In *Keep Reading*, the primary source book, pages 50–137 include articles at different levels on nature, weather, sports, and a variety of other topics.

- Articles from *Toolkit Texts*. At www.comprehensiontoolkit.com or at www.heinemann.com, you can order our *Toolkit Texts*, three volumes of short nonfiction articles on a universe of topics. We have arranged these texts by "grade level." You can choose from grades 2–3, grades 4–5, or grades 6–7, whatever meets your kids' needs.

- Additionally, seek out articles and books that relate to the content of the Toolkit lesson text or whatever social studies or science unit currently engages your class. Once kids whet their appetite for a topic, they can hardly wait to read more about it. Magazines for kids and online sources are all just a click away. We have extensive bibliographies in the Toolkits to help you find just the right text for your kids. Check out the bibliographies beginning on page 139 in *Keep Reading* in *The Primary Comprehension Toolkit* and on page 127 in *Extend and Investigate* in *The Comprehension Toolkit*, grades 3–6.

- Listings of websites containing a wealth of information and more articles begin on page 154 in *Keep Reading* in *The Primary Toolkit* and on page 138 in *Extend and Investigate* in the grades 3–6 Toolkit.

- Don't forget the books and topics you love! Passion is contagious and your kids will likely hop on board as you share text you care about.

THE INTERVENTION SESSIONS

In *Comprehension Intervention*, we have broken down the original Toolkit lessons into smaller chunks of instruction to make them more explicit and accessible. For instance, if a Toolkit lesson has three goals, we may have three separate intervention sessions to help kids meet these goals. But the intervention sessions are designed to be flexible and to target very specific comprehension needs. Sometimes our kids need all of the sessions on a specific strategy, other times one or two suffice. Kids come to the intervention sessions with some experience with the strategies that were the focus of the whole-group lesson, but our intervention highlights and revisits specific language and thinking behaviors that need additional reinforcement and practice.

Each intervention session corresponds to a specific Toolkit lesson and goals. Based on the complexity of the Toolkit lesson, we have created small-group sessions to reinforce specific parts of the Toolkit lesson. For some of the Toolkit lessons, we offer one intervention session. For others we offer as many as three or four. These multiple sessions are designed by the notation *a*, *b*, *c*, and so forth, so small-group sessions 4a and 4b are both companions to Toolkit Lesson 4. You are free to teach any or all of these based on your kids' needs.

SUMMATIVE ASSESSMENT

We have created guidelines for a summative assessment conference to target how effectively children are using the strategies as tools for understanding as they read, listen, and view. Once kids have completed all of the intervention sessions in a specific strategy and have had lots of time to practice, we suggest you use our Reading Conference protocol and recording form. This conference provides an opportunity for a more formal assessment of how your kids are using strategies to understand what they read.

SESSION WALK-THROUGH

Comprehension Intervention's four-part session supports a gradual release of responsibility from teacher to student.

1. Build Background, Word and Concept Knowledge

2. Teach/Model   **3.** Guide/Support Practice   **4.** Wrap Up

Each small-group session is identified by a numeral that matches the Toolkit lesson it follows, and, when there are multiple small-group interventions for one Toolkit lesson, a letter. So Session 3a is the first lesson for Toolkit Lesson 3; Session 3b is the second.

The first page of every session supports planning for instruction.

- **Session Goals** restate key objectives from the Toolkit launch lesson.
- **Text Matters** explains the attributes of text appropriate to this lesson and provides examples.
- **Considerations for Planning** discusses the teaching focus and key understandings as well as noting materials teachers will need to prepare for the session.

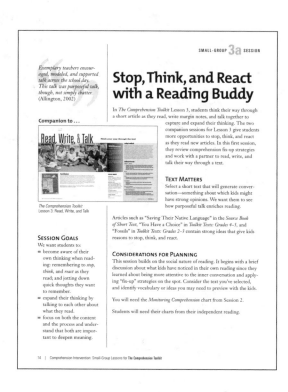

Like the Toolkit lessons, these sessions include both TEACHING MOVES, the step-by-step teaching procedure, and TEACHING LANGUAGE, the words you may use to teach key concepts to kids.

Build Background, Word and Concept Knowledge begins the session, and the teacher may:

- Connect and engage kids with the strategy
- Ask, "What do you think you know about _____?" to evaluate background content knowledge
- Provide a brief text or picture walk to preview key concepts and vocabulary
- Anticipate the hurdles that content, vocabulary, genre knowledge, decoding issues, and the like may present and troubleshoot accordingly

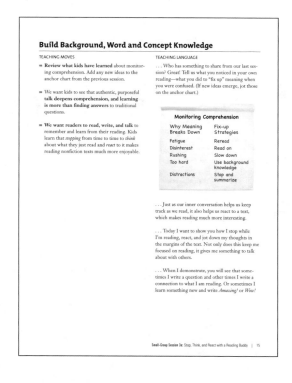

In **Teach/Model**, the teacher:

- Previews the text with kids
- Provides a brief read-aloud or think-aloud
- Explains the strategy and demonstrates how to use it

Throughout **Guide/Support Practice**, kids and teacher work together on the strategy.

- Kids and teacher read a section together; kids turn and talk; and all practice using the strategy.
- Kids read a section and use the strategy independently; teacher listens in and confers as needed.
- Kids whisper-read and use the strategy; teacher listens in, monitoring and coaching fluency and strategy use.

In **Wrap Up**, the final part of the teaching sequence, kids share and consolidate their knowledge.

- Kids share out.
- Kids and teacher summarize what was learned.
- Kids create or add to an anchor chart with the teacher.
- Kids reread for fluency practice.
- Kids go off to use the strategy with their own independent texts.

Each session ends with **Assess and Plan**, a section that supports daily progress monitoring with strategy-specific suggestions for reviewing student work, assessing students' thinking and accomplishment of session goals, and determining the need for additional practice.

A PLUG FOR READING!

Often when kids are identified as needing special help in reading, they are pulled out of the room during class reading time. What's wrong with this picture? Children who need additional support in reading should get *more* time with reading instruction, not less. They should participate fully in classroom reading instruction as well as receiving additional small-group support, either in or out of class. Kids' strategy knowledge is cumulative. As they participate in both whole-group and small-group comprehension lessons, they acquire a repertoire of strategies to use as tools for understanding. They integrate comprehension strategies as a part of their entire thinking process.

But collaborative whole-group and differentiated small-group instruction alone aren't enough. To get better at reading, kids need to log a lot of reading time in text they can and want to read. The less developed the reader, the more reading time he or she needs! Too often, the more students struggle with reading, the less time they actually get to read, partly because they are in text that is too hard for them and frequently because they are spending time on isolated skill-and-drill worksheets that provide no opportunities to read and learn. Allington (2009) suggests that students who are "behind grade level" in reading need to spend up to three times as much time reading as their grade-level peers. Kids get better at reading by reading! And reading makes them smarter, too. So give all of our kids lots of time to read, but give even more reading time to kids who need additional support. A nose in a good book is the best intervention of all!

REFERENCES

Allington, R.L. 2009. *What Really Matters in Response to Intervention: Research-Based Designs.* Boston: Pearson.

Gamse, B.C., Jacob, R.T., Horst, M., Boulay, B., and Unlu, F. 2008. Reading First Impact Study Final Report (Report No. NCEE 2009–4038). Washington, DC: National Center for Education Evaluation and Regional Assistance, Institute of Education Sciences, U. S. Department of Education.

Howard, M. 2009. *RTI from All Sides: What Every Teacher* Needs *to Know*. Portsmouth, NH: Heinemann.

Pianta, R.C., Belsky, J., Houts, R., and Morrison, F. 2007. "Opportunities to Learn in America's Elementary Classrooms." *Science* 315: 1795–1796.

Monitor Comprehension

When readers monitor their comprehension, they keep track of their thinking. They listen to the voice in their head that speaks to them as they read. They notice when the text makes sense and when it doesn't. We teach readers to "fix up" their comprehension by using a variety of strategies, including stopping to refocus thinking, rereading, and reading on.
All of the comprehension instruction in the Toolkits and *Comprehension Intervention* helps readers to monitor and use strategies to maintain understanding and repair comprehension when it breaks down.

Notice and Track Your Thinking

In *The Comprehension Toolkit* Lesson 1, students learn to listen to their inner voice and leave tracks of their thinking by jotting notes on their clipboards during a class read-aloud. This companion session offers students the opportunity to read another text in a small-group setting, using Post-its to leave tracks of their thinking right in their text.

Companion to . . .

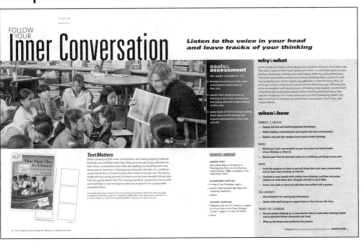

The Comprehension Toolkit
Lesson 1: Follow Your Inner
Conversation

SESSION GOALS

We want students to:

- develop an awareness of the inner conversation readers have as they read.
- monitor their comprehension by listening to their inner conversation and paying attention to their thinking as they read.
- leave tracks of their thinking by jotting down notes to hold thinking and expand understanding as they read and talk.

TEXT MATTERS

Select a text full of information that kids will find engaging and compelling. Readers are more likely to pay attention to their inner conversation when the text provokes their ideas and reactions. Be sure to select a text the kids *can* read. When the text is too difficult, too much energy goes to decoding. When it's "just right," kids have plenty of thinking energy to devote to comprehension.

A short text works well for small-group instruction. Selections like "Buried Alive!" in the *Source Book of Short Text*, "Jack Roosevelt Robinson" in *Toolkit Texts: Grades 4–5*, and "Aim for the Stars" in *Toolkit Texts: Grades 2–3* will motivate kids to pay attention to what they are thinking and learning as they read.

For independent reading, consider books like *Nettie's Trip South* by Ann Turner and *Gleam and Glow* by Eve Bunting. These work well for noticing and tracking thinking.

CONSIDERATIONS FOR PLANNING

Look through the text you have selected, and identify any vocabulary or ideas you may need to preview with the kids. Consider how much and when you will need to model and scaffold to support students' success in noticing and tracking their thinking.

Students will need Post-its.

Build Background, Word and Concept Knowledge

- **Introduce the text in a way that engages students** and activates their background knowledge. Make sure kids understand the term *background knowledge*. Readers depend on their background knowledge to connect to a text. It provides the link readers must have to understand unfamiliar concepts, language structure, text features, and words.

- **Make the text preview interactive,** inviting students to share their ideas and impressions about the text. Celebrate thinking by noticing and naming what they do.

- You'll need to **decide how much of the text to preview.** When using realistic fiction or narrative nonfiction, we preview less because we want kids to experience the story in which the important details are embedded.

- As you preview, **point out words, ideas, and concepts that might be unfamiliar.** This scaffolding during the preview allows readers to focus on thinking.

. . . I have selected a text for us to read today. I think you will like it a lot! Let me tell you a little about it . . . .

. . . Let's look to see what we can learn about this text. Turn and talk about what you notice.

. . . When we read, we think about what we already know, our *background knowledge*. All of us depend on our background knowledge to understand what we read. Nothing influences us more!

. . . So, let's think about what you already know about . . .

. . . When we think about what we already know about a concept or idea in a text before we read, it helps us better understand what we read.

. . . When we read, we make sure our goal is to understand or comprehend. Have you ever been reading along and heard a voice inside your head say, "Wow, this is interesting!" or "I never knew that!" That is your inner voice. That voice is an enormous help to us when we listen to it. When we hear it, we talk with it and call it our "inner conversation."

. . . Let's investigate a few of the words the author uses. Some of these may be unfamiliar to you, so we will take a look at them together. That way, when you read, you'll already know what the words mean, and you can think about the ideas in the text. Let's start with . . .

Teach/Model

- Explain that when we read, **we think and pay attention to our inner conversation.**

- Briefly read aloud, modeling how you think as you read. Make notes on Post-its to leave tracks of your thinking. **Show students how to record on Post-its.**

- It is helpful when modeling to **use language that kids can "borrow"** when it is time for them to respond using their own Post-its. That language might include:
  - This makes me think of . . .
  - I wonder . . .
  - This reminds me . . .
  - I didn't know that . . .
  - I learned . . .
  - I'm thinking . . .

- **Invite students to turn and talk** as you stop to share your thinking.

Teaching Tip

Since there is a high correlation between reading engagement and comprehension, be sure to build in success. If you see a text is too difficult, provide greater support through shared reading, rather than guided reading, and select an easier text for the next session.

. . . Today we will be noticing and paying careful attention to our thinking as we read.

. . . I'm going to teach you what that inner voice sounds like as we read.

. . . One way we can hold on to our thinking is by writing it on a Post-it. For example, when I read this part, it makes me wonder about . . . . Watch how I write that on a Post-it to help me remember what I was thinking when I read that part.

. . . Turn and talk about what you were thinking when I read that part. What might you have written?

. . . Talking often helps us think more deeply about what we are reading.

Guide/Support Practice

TEACHING MOVES

▪ During guided practice, share responsibility with the students to ensure success. **Do at least one more page or section together** to be sure they understand what they are to do.

▪ Guided practice is a perfect time to differentiate support. If some students show understanding, have them read on. During guided reading, we **offer students support when they need it.** This flexibility is a key component of guided reading with older students.

▪ **Notice when students aren't reading,** and provide more support. Some students need additional modeling to write a Post-it. Offer a brief model by finding a place to stop and write one together.

▪ Tell students they will read in a whisper voice and **share their thinking when you are nearby** to listen. Remind them to continue jotting their thinking on Post-its as they read.

▪ Have students share their thinking while you listen to their whisper reading. Students may need extra support, so **have some prompts ready:**
- I'm thinking . . .
- An idea I have about this . . .
- I'm wondering . . .
- I'm learning . . .

▪ Checking in quickly with individual group members will help you **determine which students might need extra support** and uncover any confusion that needs addressing.

TEACHING LANGUAGE

. . . Now it's time for you to read, too. Let's share the reading of this next part. Once you finish, write down your thinking on Post-its. Who can recall some of the things you can write?

. . . Good thinking! You can write something when your inner voice says . . .
- This makes me think of . . .
- I wonder . . .
- This reminds me . . .
- I didn't know that . . .
- I learned . . .
- I'm thinking . . .

. . . So, let's try it. (Have students read the section and write their Post-its.)

. . . Let's talk about what you wrote. (Assess to be sure students understand. If they do, let them continue.)

. . . Good! I see that Josh has written . . . (Select and celebrate things students have written that offer models.)

. . . Now it's time for you to read on your own. I will be listening to each of you. When I am nearby, I will ask you to "whisper read" (demonstrate) and think aloud when you think of something to write on a Post-it. It might sound like this: "This reminds me of . . . ."

. . . Now continue reading. Remember that thinking is an important part of reading. Listen to your inner voice, and jot your thinking on Post-its. (If the text is too long for one reading, tell students where they should stop.)

Wrap Up

TEACHING MOVES

- **Have students read and share** several of their Post-its. This is an effective and efficient way to assess both fluency and comprehension.

- **Construct an anchor chart** that captures what students recorded on their Post-its. It will serve as a reminder of both the text's content and the process.

- Students should all have an independent book they are reading. **Connect to what they have done in their small group** by giving them Post-its to use in recording something they want to remember in their independent book.

> **Teaching Tip**
> Consider at times just watching the group of readers. You can learn a great deal by watching their posture, expressions, and how quickly they turn the pages. Though fluency is surely important, we want to encourage meaningful reading, not just rapid reading.

TEACHING LANGUAGE

. . . Take just a moment and very quickly find a part where you put a Post-it. Quickly read the part and the Post-it you wrote. Who wants to start us off?

. . . Great thinking! We are going to make an anchor chart to show our thinking.

> ## Leaving Tracks of Our Thinking [Text Title]
>
> (Record students' Post-it information as they share.)

. . . Who can summarize the important work we did today? (If students need support, offer it. It is important to debrief and summarize.)

. . . All of you have an independent book you are reading. I am going to give you Post-its so you can practice recording your thinking in your own books, too!

ASSESS AND PLAN

How did students' Post-its show evidence of their thinking?

Look for evidence and consider whether re-teaching is necessary. Consider both the quality and quantity of what students write. If students aren't recording on Post-its, or the quality of what they are writing isn't useful in gaining meaning, build in more demonstration in the next session. This session includes fundamental concepts students will need. Extend the session to a second day if necessary.

Did some students need clarification?

Some students may record inaccurate information or misunderstand words or ideas. When that occurs, individually confer with students to correct and clarify misconceptions and inaccurate information.

Was the text level appropriate for students? If not, why?

If the text was not an appropriate level, select an easier or a more challenging text for the next session. Students need to spend most of their time in accessible texts.

Were there any students who would benefit from extra help?

Plan time to confer with any student who might need extra support. Done quickly, conferencing will help the student accelerate much more quickly.

What insights might you gain from the classroom teacher or others who work with the students?

Plan to check in regularly with others. The more coordination and collaboration, the better it is for the students.

Part of inviting children to notice is helping them see what kind of things might be noticed, and to name the things being noticed.
(Johnston, 2004)

Monitor and Repair Comprehension

In *The Comprehension Toolkit* Lesson 2, students notice and articulate how the teacher monitors the inner voice to focus thinking during a read-aloud, and they help create an anchor chart of fix-up strategies to use when meaning breaks down. In this companion session, students practice monitoring and fixing up comprehension as they read a text at their level.

Companion to . . .

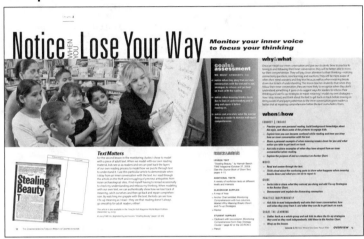

The Comprehension Toolkit
Lesson 2: Notice When You Lose Your Way

TEXT MATTERS

Select a meaningful text that will pose some obstacles for students. One advantage of small-group reading is being close at hand to offer just enough support to make readers successful. We want to coach kids in texts they are likely to encounter across the curriculum, and teach them how to depend on their inner conversations and fix-up strategies to untangle themselves when meaning breaks down.

Short texts like "Community Life" in the *Source Book of Short Text*, "War" in *Toolkit Texts: Grades 4–5*, and "Celebrating the Day of the Dead" in *Toolkit Texts: Grades 2–3* have enough information to require kids to monitor and fix up comprehension.

For independent reading, books like *Pink and Say* by Patricia Polacco or *Going Home* by Eve Bunting provide kids with good reasons for monitoring and repairing comprehension as they read.

CONSIDERATIONS FOR PLANNING

Look through the text you've selected, and identify any vocabulary or ideas you may need to preview with the kids. Consider how much and when you will need to model and scaffold to support students' success in monitoring and repairing their comprehension.

Students will need individual copies of the *Monitoring Comprehension* chart.

SESSION GOALS

We want students to:

- notice when they stray from an inner conversation with the text and to use strategies to refocus and get back on track with the reading.
- notice when meaning breaks down due to lack of understanding and to stop and repair it before reading on.
- notice and articulate what the teacher does as a reader to monitor and repair comprehension.

Build Background, Word and Concept Knowledge

- We want to **shift the responsibility to students** to pay closer attention to their reading.

- We help kids learn to **depend on their inner conversation** through our models and as-needed support. We help them learn to listen to the "signal" the voice in their head sends when a text isn't making sense.

- **Preview any unfamiliar vocabulary** so kids can focus on meaning as they read the text.

- Work with kids to **create an anchor chart** about monitoring comprehension. Record reasons why meaning may break down when we read.

. . . I have selected a text for us to read today. It will offer you lots to think about, and you will want to pay careful attention to your inner conversation as you read. As readers, we are thinking all the time and considering our understanding of the text.

. . . When I am reading, I sometimes find myself confused. My inner voice says something like, "Wait a minute!" (Use a personal story to illustrate, such as: Once I was reading an article on bedbugs. There was an enlarged picture of a bedbug, and the text said bedbugs could "grow to the size of an apple." I stopped reading and reacted. "Oh wow," I said, "that's amazing!" When I read on, I saw that it was an apple *seed*—not a whole apple!)

. . . Let's think about what causes us to stray from our inner conversation when we're reading. (Have kids suggest reasons and create an anchor chart.)

Monitoring Comprehension

Why Meaning Breaks Down	Fix-up Strategies
Fatigue	
Disinterest	
Rushing	
Too hard	
Distractions	

. . . When we read, we make sure we understand. So, in a minute, I will read aloud part of the text, and we will take a look at some of the ways we help get ourselves back on track as readers.

. . . Here are a few words you need to know . . .

Teach/Model

- We explain that when we read, we are thinking and **paying attention to our inner conversation** as an "alert system."

- Briefly read aloud, **modeling how you puzzle and problem solve** your way through a text. Notice:
  - the title
  - any unfamiliar or technical words
  - language structures that may be unusual
  - lapses in concentration

- **After the model, check** to be sure students know and understand what they are to do.

- **Have kids use a *Monitoring Comprehension* chart** as they read on. You can copy the form on page 42 of *The Comprehension Toolkit* Strategy Book 1: *Monitor Comprehension* or have students make their own charts.

Teaching Tip

Applying "fix-up" strategies at the very time meaning breaks down is efficient. Often kids just continue reading and become more and more "lost" in a text in a way that isn't good! Show students how "fixing up" comprehension along the way not only is more efficient, but also makes reading much more enjoyable.

. . . I am going to start reading the text. Watch what I do when I come to a confusing part. I'll think aloud. I want you to be ready to talk about what you notice. (Read part of the text, modeling your confusions and the fix-up strategies you use.)

. . . Turn and talk about what you saw me doing. (Add fix-up strategies to the chart.)

Monitoring Comprehension

Why Meaning Breaks Down	Fix-up Strategies
Fatigue	Reread
Disinterest	Read on
Rushing	Slow down
Too hard	Use background knowledge
Distractions	Stop and summarize

. . . Remember, fix-up strategies are what we do as readers to "fix up" or solve problems that come up as we read.

. . . Now I am going to give each of you a personal copy of the chart to use as you continue reading the text. We will talk about your problem-solving strategies—the fix-up strategies you used—after you read.

Guide/Support Practice

- Have students use the small chart to **jot down their own problem-solving strategies.**

- Since this part of the session is guided, **differentiate support.** Some readers may be less aware of meaning breaking down. Consider listening in to those readers first. If they need an extra model, read the text together and coach during the reading performance, much like an athletic coach would do to improve performance.

. . . Keep reading, and be sure to keep track of your own fix-up strategies. Jot down what you notice on your chart.

. . . I will be around to listen in.

Wrap Up

- Ask students to **share what they have written** on their charts. Add examples to the group chart.

- If the text is long, kids may not finish. You may send students on to complete the text independently. If students finish the text, **offer them a second chart** to tuck into their independent reading book.

- Tell kids they will **begin the next session by sharing** what they notice in their independent reading.

. . . Let's share what you've written on your chart. What did you notice you could do when you strayed from the inner conversation?

. . . Good thinking! Let's add that to our chart! (Add examples to the group chart. You may need to probe a bit to help kids "name" the problem and the fix-up strategies.)

. . . This isn't something we do just once or something that goes away! We all need to pay attention to our inner conversation whenever we read.

. . . I am going to give you an extra chart to put in your independent reading book. Keep track as you read and jot down what you notice. Bring that with you to our next meeting so we can share.

ASSESS AND PLAN

What kinds of things did students identify as problems, and what fix-up strategies did they use?

Look for evidence that kids are actually aware of their inner voices and have strategies for fixing up their comprehension when meaning breaks down.

Were there any students who would benefit from extra help?

Plan time to confer with any reader who might need extra support. It takes some students longer than others to "hear" the voice that helps them untangle themselves as readers. Plan to begin the next session with a discussion of what kids noticed in their continued or independent reading.

Exemplary teachers encouraged, modeled, and supported talk across the school day. This talk was purposeful talk, though, not simply chatter. (Allington, 2002)

Stop, Think, and React with a Reading Buddy

In *The Comprehension Toolkit* Lesson 3, students think their way through a short article as they read, write margin notes, and talk together to capture and expand their thinking. The two companion sessions for Lesson 3 give students more opportunities to stop, think, and react as they read new articles. In this first session, they review comprehension fix-up strategies and work with a partner to read, write, and talk their way through a text.

Companion to . . .

The Comprehension Toolkit
Lesson 3: Read, Write, and Talk

Text Matters

Select a short text that will generate conversation—something about which kids might have strong opinions. We want them to see how purposeful talk enriches reading.

Articles such as "Saving Their Native Language" in the *Source Book of Short Text*, "You Have a Choice" in *Toolkit Texts: Grades 4–5*, and "Fossils" in *Toolkit Texts: Grades 2–3* contain strong ideas that give kids reasons to stop, think, and react.

Considerations for Planning

This session builds on the social nature of reading. It begins with a brief discussion about what kids have noticed in their own reading since they learned about being more attentive to the inner conversation and applying "fix-up" strategies on the spot. Consider the text you've selected, and identify vocabulary or ideas you may need to preview with the kids.

You will need the *Monitoring Comprehension* chart from Session 2.

Students will need their charts from their independent reading.

Session Goals

We want students to:

- become aware of their own thinking when reading: remembering to *stop, think,* and *react* as they read; and jotting down quick thoughts they want to remember.

- expand their thinking by talking to each other about what they read.

- focus on both the content and the process and understand that both are important to deepen meaning.

Build Background, Word and Concept Knowledge

- **Review what kids have learned** about monitoring comprehension. Add any new ideas to the anchor chart from the previous session.

- We want kids to see that authentic, purposeful **talk deepens comprehension, and learning is more than finding answers** to traditional questions.

- **We want readers to read, write, and talk** to remember and learn from their reading. Kids learn that *stopping* from time to time to *think* about what they just read and *react* to it makes reading nonfiction texts much more enjoyable.

. . . Who has something to share from our last session? Great! Tell us what you noticed in your own reading—what you did to "fix up" meaning when you were confused. (If new ideas emerge, jot those on the anchor chart.)

Monitoring Comprehension

Why Meaning Breaks Down	Fix-up Strategies
Fatigue	Reread
Disinterest	Read on
Rushing	Slow down
Too hard	Use background knowledge
Distractions	Stop and summarize

. . . Just as our inner conversation helps us keep track as we read, it also helps us react to a text, which makes reading much more interesting.

. . . Today I want to show you how I stop while I'm reading, react, and jot down my thoughts in the margins of the text. Not only does this keep me focused on reading, it gives me something to talk about with others.

. . . When I demonstrate, you will see that sometimes I write a question and other times I write a connection to what I am reading. Or sometimes I learn something new and write *Amazing!* or *Wow!*

Teach/Model

- **Preview the text** and have kids skim and scan along with you. We want them to begin to react and consider the ideas and topic.

- Model how the stop, think, and react approach gives readers a chance to share what they are learning, pose questions, and add their own reactions and connections. This practice is an important one to carry across the curriculum. When we **model** *how to engage* in **"purposeful talk,"** we equip students for life.

- **Preview any unfamiliar vocabulary** so kids can focus on meaning as they read.

. . . We have an interesting text to read and talk about today. Let's look through it quickly together. What do you notice? What do you know about the topic?

. . . Watch as I start reading the text. I am going to put the text down on the table so you can see as I model and record my thinking.

. . . As I read, I am going to stop and record my questions, my confusions, and my reactions to my reading. (Model each of these briefly.)

. . . What are you noticing? Great! You noticed that I recorded my thinking in the margins as I read. This helps me understand what I'm reading.

. . . Turn and talk about the inner conversation you had as I was reading this part. What did you notice?

. . . Let's talk about a few words you will need to know when you read . . . .

Guide/Support Practice

TEACHING MOVES

- Ask kids to **read on in the text with a buddy** and to write their own comments, questions, and reactions in the margins.

- **Suggest that students plan** where they will stop and talk with one another.

TEACHING LANGUAGE

. . . Let's work in pairs today. Keep reading, but stop to share your thinking. Decide with your buddy how far you will read before you stop to share. Remember to use quiet voices, as we will all be in different places in the text.

. . . Write your reactions and questions in the margins of your text.

. . . I will be around to see how it's going.

Wrap Up

TEACHING MOVES

- Have students complete the reading of the text and **share their thinking.**

- Help kids **debrief their thinking** about the inner conversation and the process of jotting down their thinking as they read.

TEACHING LANGUAGE

. . . Let's share what you've written on your text.

. . . What did you notice when you stopped to talk with your buddy? (Kids will likely share that talking to someone else helped clarify thinking, helped with questions they had, or offered a different opinion or perspective on the text.)

. . . Great work today!

ASSESS AND PLAN

What kinds of things did students write on the text?
Look for evidence that kids' margin notes actually enhance and capture thinking. The students' annotations offer great insights about their understanding of both the process and the content.

Do some students need additional practice?
The next session will extend this one, offering kids more practice.

A child must have some version of, 'Yes, I imagine I can do this.' And a teacher must also view the present child as competent and on that basis imagine new possibilities. (Dyson, 1999)

Companion to . . .

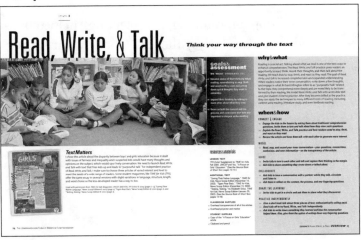

The Comprehension Toolkit
Lesson 3: Read, Write, and Talk

Session Goals

We want students to:

- become aware of their own thinking when reading: remembering to *stop*, *think*, and *react* as they read; and jotting down quick thoughts they want to remember.
- expand their thinking by talking to each other about what they read.
- focus on both the content and the process and understand that both are important to deepen meaning.

Stop, Think, and React Independently

This session follows up on the previous one. This time, kids read independently. They stop, think, and react to an article on their own, waiting until they have finished reading to talk about the content and the process.

Text Matters

Select three or four short texts from which kids can choose. Both the *Source Book of Short Text* and *Toolkit Texts: Grades 4–5* have some excellent articles from which to select options. Be sure to consider the accessibility of the texts. You want to select texts that kids can read with relative ease.

In addition to the texts listed in the previous session, selections such as "Pow Wow," "Flying High," and "Breathing Underwater" in *Toolkit Texts: Grades 2–3* may suit your readers. These offer strong ideas and intriguing information that will prompt kids to stop, think, and react during reading.

Considerations for Planning

This session connects to the previous one and offers kids another opportunity to read, write, and talk. Most of the time is devoted to kids actually reading the text and then talking about their experience of recording their thinking in the margins.

You will need several copies of each article in case kids all choose the same one.

Build Background, Word and Concept Knowledge

TEACHING MOVES

■ **Review what kids did in the previous session.**

■ **Have students share** how the practice of "stop, think, and react" enhanced their understanding and their enjoyment of reading. We want kids to see that though we often read independently, our "talk" inside our heads and with other people always enriches reading.

TEACHING LANGUAGE

. . . Take a moment to turn and talk about the reading and thinking we did during our last session.

. . . Right! We recorded our inner conversation as we read, and we also talked to our buddies to share our thinking. Sometimes we asked a question, made a connection, or reacted to the information.

. . . "Stopping, thinking, and reacting" helped us understand and enjoy the text. Today we are going to continue to do that.

Teach/Model

TEACHING MOVES

■ **Display enough copies** of each text that all students could select the same one.

■ Offer a brief, engaging **preview of each text.**

■ Explain to students that this time they will **read and write on their own,** waiting to share their thinking until after they have finished.

TEACHING LANGUAGE

. . . Let me share some really interesting texts I selected. Today you will have a choice.

. . . I want to tell you a little about each one. Listen and see which is most interesting to you.

. . . Now you have a choice to make. Select the article you want to read.

. . . We will do the same thing we did in our last session. You will record your thinking and your inner conversation in the margins. This time, however, we will wait to talk about our thinking until after we have read our article and jotted down our thoughts in the margins.

Guide/Support Practice

TEACHING MOVES

- Ask kids to **read the text independently** and to write their own comments, questions, and reactions right on the text.

- As you **check in with kids,** offer help with vocabulary words, as needed, so they focus on meaning as they read and react.

TEACHING LANGUAGE

. . . Let's work independently today.

. . . Everyone has an article selected. Start reading and writing your comments, questions, and reactions in the margins.

. . . I will be around to see how it's going.

Wrap Up

TEACHING MOVES

- When students have completed their reading, **invite them to share their thinking.** (It is possible some will not finish, but all will have something to share.)

- **If more than one student selected a text** and time permits, you might have them turn and talk first with someone who also read the same text. Then have the pairs share.

TEACHING LANGUAGE

. . . Let's share! What did you notice about your reading today? (Listen to kids' sharing to see if the process of "stop, think, and react" was easier this second time.)

. . . Remember, even when you are reading in your own independent books and your science or social studies books, you can talk to others about what you are noticing as you read. You can use Post-its to capture your thinking.

. . . Great work today!

ASSESS AND PLAN

Did students seem more comfortable with the "stop, think, and react" process?

Look at kids' margin notes and reflect on their sharing to determine whether the process felt more natural. If not, offer additional opportunities to practice. Using short, interesting texts not only offers kids more practice, but also gives us insights about how their thinking develops during reading. We glean important information for planning future sessions when we carefully assess students' margin notes and discussion contributions.

Reading Conference
Monitor Comprehension

After this unit, you want to know that students are consciously making meaning, so your conference should help the student talk about both the process and the content of reading: what he or she was thinking while reading.

1. **Invite the student to choose a passage and create a context for it.**
   - Choose a part of your book to read to me.
   - Tell me what you were thinking when you read that part.

2. **Focus in on monitoring strategies by prompting the student to talk about the text and his or her written or drawn responses.**
   - Listen to your inner conversation. What are you thinking? What do you wonder? What did you learn?
   - Show me something you drew or wrote about your reading. Tell me about it.
   - Why do you stop and think when you are reading rather than speed right through? How does that help you as a reader?

3. **Determine the student's knowledge of fix-up strategies.**
   - Did you find anything confusing in the part you read? Did you figure it out? How?
   - Read it to me again and let's figure it out together. What can we do to help ourselves? *(Reread. Read on. Slow down. Use background knowledge. Stop and summarize. Talk to someone.)*

Reading Conference Recording Form: Monitor Comprehension	
Name _____ Date _____	
Book title _____	
GOAL	**EVIDENCE**
The student . . .	This student . . .
1. Understands the text • Tells what the book is about and talks about what she or he was thinking while reading	
2. Is aware of his or her own monitoring strategies • Responds to text while reading, for example, wondering about content, relating it to something he or she knows, noting when she or he doesn't understand • Jots down thoughts and reactions to reading	
3. Knows fix-up strategies for regaining meaning • Explains what to do when she or he doesn't understand part of the text	

©2010 by Stephanie Harvey, Anne Goudvis, and Judy Wallis. From *Comprehension Intervention: Small-Group Lessons for The Comprehension Toolkit.* Portsmouth, NH: Heinemann. This page may be copied for classroom use only.

Conference Recording Form for "Monitor Comprehension," located in "Resources" section.

Language students may use to demonstrate that they are monitoring meaning

- I am thinking . . . The story makes me think about . . .
- I am having an inner conversation . . . My inner voice says . . .
- I don't get it . . . I don't understand . . . This doesn't make sense . . . Huh? I don't get this part . . .
- Oh, now I get it (after rereading, reading on, talking and discussion) . . .
- I understand . . . I learned . . .

Follow-ups

If a student has difficulty with any of the primary goals in this unit, prompts like the following may be helpful during independent work in subsequent units.

- What are you thinking?
- What are you hearing in your inner conversation?
- Are you listening to your inner voice?
- Does this remind you of anything? What?
- Any questions?
- What were your reactions? Were you surprised? Amazed?
- How can you keep track of what you want to remember in this book?
- You look puzzled about that part. How can you fix up that problem?

Activate and Connect

The background knowledge we bring to our reading colors every aspect of our learning and understanding. Whether we are questioning, inferring, or synthesizing, our background knowledge is the foundation of our thinking. We simply can't understand what we read without thinking about what we already know.

Readers must connect the new to the known. Sometimes, however, our prior knowledge consists of misconceptions that get in the way of new learning. So we have to prepare kids not only to think about what they already know, but also to change their thinking when they encounter new and more accurate information.

> *We learn from our students that the drive to read, to digest, to reread, and to build connections with nonfiction is meaningful, stimulating, and powerful.* (Hill and Budka, 2009)

Companion to . . .

The Comprehension Toolkit
Lesson 4: Follow the Text Signposts

Explore Visual and Text Features

In *The Comprehension Toolkit Lesson 4*, students explore nonfiction features in an array of texts and make a *Feature/Purpose* anchor chart. The two companion sessions for Lesson 4 offer students more practice and support for using nonfiction features to guide their learning. In this first session, students look through a variety of texts and create a *Visual Features/ Text Features* anchor chart. Then they identify features in a selected text.

TEXT MATTERS

Gather a variety of nonfiction books, magazines, and articles that have both visual and text features, so kids see how to use both types of features to navigate text. Include examples of features kids are likely to encounter in their textbook reading, such as charts and indexes. Books by Franklyn Branley, Seymour Simon, and Stephen Kramer include lots of features. *National Geographic Explorer* articles fairly burst with features.

Choose a short text to read with the kids. "Tigers Roar Back" in the *Source Book of Short Text* and "Where Do I Live," "Riding the Rails," and "From Egg to Salamander" in *Toolkit Texts: Grades 2–3* offer a variety of features to explore.

SESSION GOALS

We want students to:
- identify features.
- gain accurate information from features as they encounter them in their reading.

CONSIDERATIONS FOR PLANNING

Display the books, magazines, and articles that show different visual and text features. Be sure to consider students' ages and needs as you select the features. Limit the number and types of features accordingly.

One key understanding to explore in this session is how both visual and text features contribute to the reader's understanding of information in the text.

Plan to create a *Visual Features/Text Features* anchor chart, which you will build with the kids during instruction.

Students will need Post-its for this session.

Build Background, Word and Concept Knowledge

TEACHING MOVES

■ Invite kids to **look through the nonfiction texts** you've gathered. After they've had a moment to explore, begin to share the text you are looking through. Model the language you'll want kids to use: "Wow! Look at this . . ."; "I never knew that . . ."; "I wonder . . . ."

■ Have kids **name some of the features** they are noticing. If they aren't sure what word to use, offer the appropriate name. You may want to put a Post-it on each text and have students list some of the features in that particular text.

■ Remind kids that nonfiction includes features that help them navigate the text and learn information. **Introduce the terms *visual features* and *text features*.**

■ Helping kids **use correct terms** enriches their learning and offers them ways to talk about features in their reading and use them in their writing.

TEACHING LANGUAGE

. . . Let's take a look at all these great nonfiction texts! Everyone, grab a text to explore. We will spend a few minutes looking through them to see what is included.

. . . I'm noticing . . . Wow! Look at this . . . (Share a few responses to the text you will be reading with the kids.)

. . . Turn and talk about what you are noticing.

. . . Today we are going to explore nonfiction features. Nonfiction features are like signposts; they help us find our way through the text. Reading nonfiction includes using lots of features that give us information about a topic. We need to know what the features are and what purposes they serve in helping us learn and understand the information.

. . . There are two big categories, or types, of features. When we look at illustrations, we can see they "picture" something. We call these *visual features*. Visual features include things like photographs, diagrams, and close-ups. Other features, like labels and captions, are made up of words. We call these *text features*. As readers, we use both visual and text features to learn more and understand more!

. . . Turn and talk about the two types of features.

Teach/Model

- Have students **think about all the features they noticed.** If you used Post-its to record on the covers of the texts, have kids use those Post-its to name the features. As needed, offer kids the correct terms for the features.

- **Create a *Visual Features/Text Features* chart** and sort features kids noticed in all the texts.

- **Preview the short text** kids will read. Introduce pertinent vocabulary.

- To model how a reader uses the features, **read a section or page,** showing how you move from connected text to the features and back again. One of the most challenging tasks for a reader is navigating back and forth between the connected text and the features.

. . . So, the visual and text features we are learning to use include many kinds of features. Let's make an anchor chart to help us remember some of the features we just noticed.

. . . Turn and talk about what we might include. (Create a chart like this one, including any of the features kids noticed in the books.)

Visual Features	Text Features
photographs	bold print
illustrations	captions on photographs
drawings	titles
charts	headings
graphs	index
maps	table of contents

. . . I am going to show you how I use the features in the text we will read today. Watch how I use the features to learn and understand information. (Model how you learn information from specific features.)

. . . Turn and talk about what you are noticing.

. . . I'm going to use Post-its to label some of the features I am using.

. . . Let's talk about some words you'll need to know when you read . . .

Guide/Support Practice

- Have kids continue reading in their copy of the text, **using Post-its to label the features.**

- Explain that **if they don't know the correct name** of the feature, they can just put an arrow on the Post-it to point to the feature they noticed.

- Examples of each feature can be added to the chart to **support kids in linking the name with each feature.**

. . . Now you read on. I will give you Post-its to put on the features you find. You can write what the feature is or just draw an arrow to point to it. After you've read a few more pages, we'll talk about what you found.

. . . I will be around to listen to your reading.

. . . Who can explain your task? Great!

Wrap Up

- Have kids identify the features they found and **talk about what they learned** from each.

- Encourage students to **look for interesting examples of features** in newspapers or magazines they may find at home. As they bring in examples, you can create a chart that everyone can add to.

. . . Who wants to share a feature you found and tell us what you learned from it?

. . . You did a good job identifying these features and sharing what you learned. Next time we meet, we will talk more about the features and the purposes they serve. Leave your Post-its in your text for our next session.

. . . Let's be on the lookout for interesting features we see in magazines and newspapers. We can all bring them in and create a class "features" chart.

ASSESS AND PLAN

Did some students seem distracted rather than supported by the features?

The more features a text contains, the more chance there is for the reader to be challenged in using them. Additional demonstrations about navigating back and forth among the features and the connected text, integrating information, will help students become more familiar and adept with this process.

Do you notice students navigating similar features in their textbooks?

Consider using examples from students' science and social studies textbooks. This not only offers additional examples, but also helps kids transfer what they are learning about visual and text features.

> *Teaching students how to learn is powerful because when they realize that the strategies lead to knowledge and that knowledge is exciting, they will communicate this knowledge to others.*
> (Swan, 2003)

Identify Purposes of Visual and Text Features

This session builds on the previous one. Students chart the purposes for the features they found in the text and record information they learn from the features.

Companion to . . .

The Comprehension Toolkit
Lesson 4: Follow the Text Signposts

SESSION GOALS

We want students to:
- identify features and describe their purposes— how they help us understand information, concepts, and ideas.
- gain accurate information from features as they encounter them in their reading.
- understand how text and visual features complement each other.

TEXT MATTERS

It is important to surround students with all kinds of nonfiction texts that include a variety of features. You can keep them in baskets arranged by topics, authors, or even features, such as indexes, charts, or illustrations. Since small-group instruction is focused and intense, be sure to provide kids with opportunities for exploring all kinds of nonfiction texts.

Continue with the text used in the previous session.

CONSIDERATIONS FOR PLANNING

We deepen kids' knowledge of features in this second session, helping them determine the purpose of each feature.

As you model in the same text, reinforce the name of the feature as you add its purpose. Be prepared to make a *Feature/Purpose/What I Learned* chart.

Students will need their texts with Post-its from the previous session.

Have on hand the *Visual Features/Text Features* anchor chart from the previous session.

Build Background, Word and Concept Knowledge

- Invite kids to **look back through the text** and recall the features they noted.

- Help kids use the correct names for the features and **note whether they are visual or text features.**

. . . Let's look back at the text we read last time. Turn and talk about some of the features you noticed.

. . . Remember, there are two categories of features: *visual features* and *text features*. We found and used both in our reading. Who can identify a visual feature? Who can identify a text feature?

. . . Today we will learn the purpose of the features—the specific ways they help us.

Teach/Model

- To model how a reader uses the features, **read a few pages and think aloud** for kids as you move from connected text to the features and back again. One of the most challenging tasks for a reader is navigating back and forth.

- Begin a *Feature/Purpose/What I Learned* **chart** for the text.

- Have students **think about all the features they noticed.** Refer back to the chart from the previous session to help kids identify and name each feature.

- **Discuss the purpose of each of the features.**

. . . I'm going to reread a page or two. Listen as I think aloud about each feature's purpose.

. . . Let's make a chart to show the purpose features serve as we read. How does each of these features help us understand what we read? (Begin adding a purpose for each feature you found in the previous session. Charts will vary to show the features in the selected text.)

. . . I'm going to add a note or two about what I learned from the features in this part.

Feature	Purpose	What I Learned
Visual Features		
photographs, illustrations, drawings	show us what something looks like	(a statement of information learned)
charts, graphs	arrange information	
maps	show locations	
Text Features		
bold print		
captions on photographs		
titles		
headings		
indexes		
table of contents		

Guide/Support Practice

- **Have kids reread** in the text (and finish it if they didn't during the previous session).

- **Add the purpose of the feature and what they learned from it to the Post-its** that label the features.

. . . Reread the text. As you come to a Post-it labeling a feature, think about what that feature helps you learn from the text and jot it on the Post-it. (You may want to have students read a page or two and share out what they learned to be sure they understand their task before they continue independently.)

. . . I will be around to listen to your reading.

Wrap Up

- Have kids discuss features and their purposes, **adding to the chart.**

- Invite students to **share the information** they learned from the features.

. . . Let's talk about what you discovered and add the purpose and the information you learned to our chart. (Have students look back through the text and then add to the chart.)

. . . Who can share the information you learned from one of these features? Who has a purpose to add to one of the features? (Have students continue to look back and explain the purposes. Offer support as needed.)

. . . You discovered lots about how features teach us so much and make reading more interesting!

ASSESS AND PLAN

Did students grasp the purpose features serve?

If some features seemed more challenging than others, continue to provide examples for students to explore. Emphasize what we can learn from particular features and how they support us to better understand the text.

Listen for Language that Signals New Learning

In *The Comprehension Toolkit* Lesson 5, students think about new information and listen for the language that signals new learning as they respond to a read-aloud book about lightning. This companion session for Lesson 5 offers students an opportunity to practice listening to their inner voice and recognizing the language that signals new learning as they read a shorter text.

TEXT MATTERS

Merging their background knowledge with new information is challenging for kids. For this session we want to select a text that is interesting and engaging and has features from which kids might also learn.

Companion to . . .

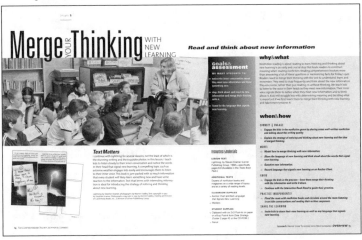

The Comprehension Toolkit
Lesson 5: Merge Your Thinking with New Learning

Texts that work well include "Hard at Work" and "One Bad Bug" in the *Source Book of Short Text*, "Mexico" in *Toolkit Texts: Grades 2–3*, and "The Long Swim" in *Toolkit Texts: Grades 4–5*. These have features that help kids make connections to new information.

CONSIDERATIONS FOR PLANNING

As kids read nonfiction, we help them become aware of their inner voice that signals new information. Reading nonfiction requires the reader to stop, think about, and react to new learning. We help kids see how new information is merged with existing knowledge by taking time to process and integrate it.

SESSION GOALS

We want students to:

- notice the inner conversation when they meet new information and learn something new.
- stop, think about, and react to new information and merge their thinking with it.
- listen for the language that signals new learning.

Look through the text you have selected and note vocabulary words or concepts to preview or review quickly with students.

Students will need Post-its for this session.

Build Background, Word and Concept Knowledge

- **Engage kids in a discussion of the text.** Show how the author has organized the text to help the reader learn. Preview features that have been discussed in the previous session, explaining that the features, too, are a great source of new information.

- Point out and quickly **discuss unfamiliar vocabulary.**

- **Explain how we notice and think about new learning** and how we merge or integrate it with what we already know.

Teaching Tip

Be sure to consider students' interests and experiences when selecting texts. We want kids to activate their background knowledge and pay attention to the inner conversation that signals they have learned something new.

. . . Let's look at this text. I think you will find it really interesting. Think about what you already know about the topic.

. . . If there are some words or ideas that are unfamiliar, we can talk about those . . . .

. . . We have been talking about how authors of nonfiction help us by including both visual and text features. Turn and talk about some of the features you notice in this text.

. . . What do you notice? Who wants to share?

. . . When we read nonfiction, we almost always learn something new. When we learn something new, we merge or combine that new information with what we already know. Often that means we slow down a bit as we read so we can think about what we already know. Also, we usually *react* to what we are reading and learning. That means we really think about it. We get excited, surprised, happy, sad, or sometimes even mad.

. . . Today we will learn how to recognize that we have encountered something new by listening to our inner conversation as we read.

Teach/Model

- **Show students how you read,** noting new information and merging it with what you know.

- **Model using Post-its** to take notes and code new learning with an *L*.

- **Create an anchor chart** to show the language that signals new learning.

. . . I want to show you something really important today—how to listen to your inner conversation when you read new information. I stop, think, and react when I hear words like . . .

- "No way!"
- "I never knew that!"

. . . Let me show you how it works. I'm going to read a bit of the text and think aloud for you as I read.

. . . Here is something I never knew! I am going to put a Post-it right beside that new information. I will write on the Post-it what I heard in my head as I read: *I never knew . . .* , and I will code it with an *L* for *learned.* (Continue to read and model just long enough to show students how they will do it.)

. . . Turn and talk about what you see me doing. (Have students respond.)

. . . Let's create an anchor chart to show how our inner voice signals new learning.

Language that Signals New Learning

- I never knew . . .
- Wow!

. . . And here's something else my inner voice says: *I used to think . . .* , *but now I know . . . .* This language shows that our thinking can change as we learn new information.

. . . Now it's time for you to try the same thing.

Guide/Support Practice

- **Have kids read the text, adding Post-its** that identify new information.

- **Have kids add to the Post-its** what they hear their inner voice saying.

. . . I am going to give you some Post-its. When you read some information that is new, use a Post-it to note your new learning and what you hear your inner voice saying. Be sure to write only one new idea per Post-it.

. . . I will be around to listen to your reading.

Wrap Up

TEACHING MOVES

- Have kids **discuss what they wrote** on their Post-its.

- **Add any new language** to the anchor chart.

- Have students share their thinking. **If they have difficulty,** offer some examples to help them reflect.

TEACHING LANGUAGE

. . . Turn and talk about what you heard your inner voice saying when you read new information.

. . . Let's look back at our anchor chart to see if we can add any new language.

Language that Signals New Learning

- I never knew . . .
- Wow!
- I learned . . .
- I was surprised by . . .
- I can't believe . . .
- Amazing!

. . . Great thinking! As you read and identified new information, you merged that new information with what you already knew.

. . . There are lots of great nonfiction books. You can try this with other texts! Keep listening for the inner voice that tells you you're learning.

ASSESS AND PLAN

Did students recognize and record new learning?
If students recorded very little, they may need additional practice listening and responding to their inner conversation. Offer additional support by modeling and conferring with kids individually.

Make sure students are using strategies from this as well as previous sessions:

- monitoring comprehension and using fix-up strategies
- noticing and gaining information from features
- merging their thinking with new information and using language that signals new learning

> *Nothing colors our thinking more than what we bring to it.* (Harvey and Goudvis, 2007)

Companion to . . .

The Comprehension Toolkit
Lesson 6: Connect the New
to the Known

Activate Background Knowledge

In *The Comprehension Toolkit* Lesson 6, students use a *What I Know/ What I Learned* chart to record their background knowledge, add to their knowledge base, and clear up misconceptions as they react to an article about sharks. The two sessions supporting Lesson 6 help kids break down this process as they read another text. In this first session, they focus on identifying their background knowledge and new learning on another chart: *What I Think I Know/What I Learned.*

TEXT MATTERS

For this session we want to select a text featuring a topic about which kids have some background knowledge, but one that also contains some opportunity for new learning.

Books by Seymour Simon or Steven Kramer offer a range of topics and include many engaging features. Nonfiction reading is like a slideshow; we can choose to read a few pages rather than reading an entire text.

Short texts also work well, such as "Understanding Electricity" in the *Source Book of Short Text*, "Firefighting through the Ages" in *Toolkit Texts: Grades 4–5*, and "Animal Helpers" or "Exploring Our Forests" in *Toolkit Texts: Grades 2–3*. These offer new information on topics about which kids will have some background knowledge.

CONSIDERATIONS FOR PLANNING

We want to show kids that our background knowledge influences everything we read. We use our past experiences and the information we know about a topic to make sense of what we are reading. This is particularly true in nonfiction. We activate our knowledge and use it as we add to it.

Students will need Post-its for this session.

SESSION GOALS

We want students to:
- understand that what readers learn depends on what they already know or don't know.
- recognize that thinking about what they already know will help them understand new information.

Build Background, Word and Concept Knowledge

- **Engage kids in a discussion of the text.** Create interest about the topic by telling kids why you selected it and asking what they already know about it.

- Explain how we notice and think about new learning and **connect it with what we already know.**

- Stress the idea that our background knowledge is **"what we *think* we know."** This prepares kids to change or add to their knowledge if they have inaccurate information.

- **Preview any vocabulary** that may be unfamiliar to facilitate kids' comprehension of the text.

. . . Let's look at this text. It is so interesting.

. . . I bet you already know something about . . . Turn and talk about something you already know.

. . . Who wants to share what you think you know about this topic?

. . . Readers keep what they *think* they already know about a topic in their mind as they read a text about that topic. As we read, we think about how the new information connects to what we already know.

. . . Sometimes when we read, we find information that is different from our background knowledge. We realize that our background knowledge wasn't quite *accurate*, or correct, and we change it.

Teaching Tip
Be sure to consider students' background experiences when selecting texts. It is important that they bring some background knowledge to the reading.

Teach/Model

- Show students how you **activate your background knowledge** and add it to the anchor chart.

- Explain how you **listen to your inner voice** as you read.

- Read enough of the text to **provide an example of learning** that adds to your knowledge and an example of learning that changes your thinking. Make sure kids know and understand what they are to do.

. . . Today as I read, I am going to think about what I already know. Watch how I use that background information.

. . . I am going to make a chart with two columns: *What I Think I Know* and *What I Learned.*

What I Think I Know	What I Learned

. . . I'll jot what I already know in the first column, *What I Think I Know.* As I read, I will add information to the other column, *What I Learned.* Sometimes when I learn new information, my thinking changes. What I learn may add to or change what I know.

. . . Listen as I read. I am going to stop from time to time to share information that is new for me. I will listen for my inner voice to signal me. (Read a bit.) Wow! I already knew . . . , and now I have added to my knowledge. I'll write my new learning in the *What I Learned* column. (Demonstrate how you note and record new information.)

. . . This is interesting! I wrote down what I thought I knew about . . . . But now my thinking has changed because I learned something new. So now I know . . .

. . . Turn and talk about what you notice.

Guide/Support Practice

TEACHING MOVES

- **Have kids read the text,** using Post-its to record their new learning. If the text is long, students may continue reading in the following session.

> **Teaching Tip**
>
> You may decide to have students use individual charts instead of using Post-its. A form for copying can be found on page 43 of *The Comprehension Toolkit* Strategy Book 2: *Activate and Connect*. Students can also make their own *What I Think I Know/What I Learned* charts.

TEACHING LANGUAGE

. . . I am going to give you some Post-its. As you read and find some information that is new to you, use a Post-it to identify what you learned. We will add the information to our anchor chart when we finish reading.

. . . I will be around to listen to your reading.

Wrap Up

TEACHING MOVES

- Have kids **discuss what they learned and add it to the chart.** Students can use their Post-its to make personal charts.

- **Reinforce for kids** that when we activate our prior knowledge, it makes reading about a topic not only easier but also much more satisfying and productive.

- Ask kids to think about the ideas recorded on the chart. Have students **think about what ideas are worth remembering** and adding to their own background knowledge.

- **Keep the anchor chart** for the next session.

TEACHING LANGUAGE

. . . Turn and talk about any new information you learned.

. . . Let's record the new information we learned on our anchor chart under *What I Learned*.

What I Think I Know	What I Learned

. . . So, you see how great it is to start with what you know. When you do, you are much more likely to hear your inner voice when it signals you've just read something you never knew. That makes it easier to add what you are learning to what you already know.

. . . Let's take a look at our chart and see if there is some information worth remembering. Who would like to share what you added to your knowledge about (topic)?

ASSESS AND PLAN

Did students recognize the importance of thinking first about what they know?

Another way to reinforce for kids the importance of thinking first about what they know is by connecting or organizing information into categories. Write a big idea in a circle and then add linked ideas in two colors: one color for what kids knew and another for what they learned. This helps kids see and understand that they are building networks of knowledge they will use and add to over and over again.

> *We tend to respond and talk back to nonfiction texts more than to other texts, and it is helpful to encourage children to do this.* (Calkins, 2001)

Clear Up Misconceptions

This session builds on the previous one. Students clear up misconceptions in their background knowledge as they continue reading and connecting new learning to what they thought they knew.

TEXT MATTERS

Continue using the text from the previous session. If readers didn't complete the text, they will read on. If they finished, they will reread for a different purpose in this session.

CONSIDERATIONS FOR PLANNING

Since our background knowledge influences our reading, its accuracy or inaccuracy also impacts our reading. All readers form misconceptions. Some are simply incorrect generalizations, while others are rooted in misinformation we have heard or read. Whatever the case, it is important to identify our misconceptions and clear them up so we have accurate information.

We help kids see that they may have misconceptions in their thinking, and we show them how to watch for information that changes their thinking.

You will need the *What I Think I Know/What I Learned* anchor chart from the previous session.

Students will need Post-its for this session.

Companion to . . .

The Comprehension Toolkit
Lesson 6: Connect the New to the Known

SESSION GOALS

We want students to:
- recognize that some of their background knowledge is inaccurate.
- realize that reading can clear up misconceptions and change thinking.

Build Background, Word and Concept Knowledge

TEACHING MOVES

- Look back over the text from the previous session and the anchor chart. **Discuss what kids knew and learned** so they see how much they expanded on their background knowledge.

- Explain that **sometimes we have inaccurate information** in our background knowledge. Our *misconceptions* may include: misinterpreting information, hearing or reading something inaccurate, or having an incomplete understanding.

- When we read, **we sometimes have to change our thinking** to correct our misconceptions and understandings.

TEACHING LANGUAGE

. . . Let's look back over the text we just read and our chart.

. . . Turn and talk about what you knew before reading and the information you learned as you read.

. . . Sometimes our background knowledge includes *misconceptions*. A misconception is a misunderstanding, often some information that is not accurate. We might hear or read something that is inaccurate. We might misunderstand the information. Or we might simply not know enough about a topic to have accurate information. But when we learn new information, it's important that it's accurate information.

. . . We all have misconceptions, and through reading and listening we often identify them ourselves and change our thinking as we correct them.

Teach/Model

- Make sure students understand that **we all have misconceptions,** and reading new information and paying close attention to it often clears up our misunderstanding.

- **Revisit the anchor chart** to check for misconceptions.

- Explain how you **listen to your inner voice** as you reread or read on.

. . . Today we will reread (or read on) in our text to see if some of what we learn actually changes something we thought we knew.

. . . First, let's look at the *What I Learned* side of our anchor chart. Right here, I see something that cleared up a misconception I had. I used to think . . . , but now I have more information. So now I know . . . .

. . . Does anyone see something that cleared up a misconception you had? Turn and talk. (Have kids share if they had a misconception.)

. . . I am going to reread (or read on in) the text. I will share my inner conversation so you can see how I clear up any misconceptions I have. (Read or reread the text, sharing your thinking.)

. . . Turn and talk about what you notice.

. . . Now I want you to do the same thing. Write what you learned on a Post-it, and also record any change in your thinking.

Guide/Support Practice

TEACHING MOVES

- **If kids are reading on** in the text, have them use Post-its to record new learning and misconceptions that they clear up.

- **If kids are rereading,** have them note any misconceptions their reading clears up.

TEACHING LANGUAGE

. . . Who can tell us what our task is?

. . . Great!

. . . I will be around to support your reading.

Wrap Up

TEACHING MOVES

- **Have kids share** their misconceptions.

- **Create a new chart:** *What I Thought/ Now I Know.* Ask kids to think about how they expanded and changed their own background knowledge as they read the text.

TEACHING LANGUAGE

. . . Turn and talk about any misconceptions you identified and any new information you learned as you read.

. . . Let's make a new chart to show how we changed our thinking and made our background knowledge more accurate.

What I Thought	Now I Know . . .

. . . Wow! You did lots of good thinking and changed your background knowledge in two ways: you added to it and you cleared up misconceptions.

ASSESS AND PLAN

Did students recognize misconceptions in their background knowledge?
This is a challenging concept. As kids have more experience, they will be more alert to misconceptions. Modeling this in content-area discussions is one way to expand students' awareness. You may also have them read another text on a similar topic for additional practice building on their knowledge and clearing up misconceptions.

During reading, check to make sure students are:
- monitoring their understanding and leaving tracks of their thinking.
- gaining information from visual and text features.
- using language that signals new learning, such as "Wow! I never knew . . . .

Reading Conference

Activate and Connect

After this unit, you want to know that students are consciously using what they know to make sense of new information, so your conference should help the student talk about his or her background knowledge and show she or he understands new information.

1. **Invite the student to choose a passage and create a context for it.**
   - Choose a part of your book to read to me.
   - Tell me what it's about.
   - What did you know about this before you read this part? How did that help you understand it?

2. **Focus on getting information from visual and text features.**
   - *(If the student is reading nonfiction with visual or text features—photos, diagrams, charts, bold print, headings, etc.)* Show me a text or visual feature and tell me about the information it gives you.
   - What is the purpose of a photograph (illustration, chart, graph, map, caption, title, heading, index, table of contents, bold print)?

3. **Ask the student to relate background knowledge to new learning.**
   - Share a spot where you read something that confirmed what you already knew.
   - Show me a part where you learned something new and share a reaction you had to that.
   - Show me something you wrote or drew that shows how you merged your thinking with the information.

4. **Discuss using new information to correct inaccurate prior knowledge.**
   - Did you have the wrong idea about something? What did you learn that changed your mind?

Reading Conference Recording Form: Activate and Connect

Name _____ Date _____

Book title _____

GOAL	EVIDENCE
The student . . .	**This student . . .**
1. Understands the text • Tells what the book is about and what he or she learned by reading it	
2. Notices and uses text and visual features • Identifies text and visual features and talks about the information he or she learned from them • Explains the purpose of features	Note: Use only if the student is reading nonfiction with visual/text features.
3. Uses background knowledge to understand new information • Notices and reacts when the text confirms something she or he already knew • Uses language that signals new learning	
4. Identifies inaccurate prior knowledge and changes thinking based on new information • Tells how new information cleared up a misconception	

©2010 by Stephanie Harvey, Anne Goudvis, and Judy Wallis. From *Comprehension Intervention: Small-Group Lessons for The Comprehension Toolkit*. Portsmouth, NH: Heinemann. This page may be copied for classroom use only.

Conference Recording Form for "Activate and Connect," located in "Resources" section.

Follow-Ups

If the student has difficulty with any of the primary goals in this unit, prompts like the following may be helpful during independent work in subsequent units.

- What do you already know about this topic?
- What does this remind you of?
- Did you remember to merge your thinking?
- What do you hear in your inner conversation?
- What did you learn?
- What do you wonder?
- Did anything you read change your mind?

Language students may use to demonstrate that they are using their background knowledge to connect new information to what they already know

- This reminds me of . . .
- I know . . .
- I noticed . . .
- I never knew . . .
- I learned . . .
- That changes my mind . . .
- I used to think . . . Now I think . . .
- That feature helps me understand . . .

Ask Questions

Questions are at the heart of teaching and learning. They open the doors to understanding the world. Posing questions allows us to seek out information, solve problems, and extend our understanding. As we try to answer our questions, we discover new information and gain new knowledge.

Especially when we read nonfiction, our questions abound. Our questions help us clarify confusion when we meet unfamiliar information, concepts, and vocabulary. The best questions spark more questions and spur further research and inquiry. They propel us to read on and find the answers. Questions nudge curious minds to investigate.

> *Good readers question and challenge authors as they read.* (Block and Pressley, 2002)

Note Questions and Answers While Reading

In *The Comprehension Toolkit* Lesson 7, students learn to ask questions and look for answers using a variety of strategies as they share a narrative nonfiction read-aloud. The two sessions supporting Lesson 7 help kids break down this process. In this first session, students record questions they have and answers they find as they read another text.

Companion to . . .

The Comprehension Toolkit
Lesson 7: Question the Text

TEXT MATTERS

Questions often arise in the midst of new learning. Select a text that has intriguing concepts and information that will engage your young readers, provoke their questions, and give them much to wonder about.

Short texts like "Hurricane Hunters" in the *Source Book of Short Text* and "Shadows" and "Flying Again" in *Toolkit Texts: Grades 2–3* work well. These provide enough facts to stimulate kids' questions.

CONSIDERATIONS FOR PLANNING

Questioning has often been seen as an "after-reading" add-on in comprehension instruction, but we now know that providing readers opportunities to ask questions before, during, and after reading is critical. It is often the questions we ask that help us organize and integrate new information and drive us to continue reading and investigating.

Asking questions about unfamiliar words can help students look more efficiently for context clues to unlock meaning.

Students will need Post-its for this session.

SESSION GOALS

We want students to:
- ask questions as they read and understand that good readers question the text.
- stop and notice when their questions are answered.

Build Background, Word and Concept Knowledge

- **Explain how questioning fuels our reading.** Make sure kids understand the difference between a question such as we are asked on a test and an authentic question—one we wonder about and are really curious about!

- **Show the title** of the article or the cover of the book you've selected, and let kids turn and talk to share the questions they have.

- **Preview vocabulary** words that will support kids to understand the text.

> **Teaching Tip**
>
> Many students are used to questions that have immediate right or wrong answers. We want kids to learn to use their questions as a means to further understanding, not as an end in and of themselves.

. . . As readers, we wonder about all sorts of things as we read. Often we think that questions are what *someone else* asks and we have to answer! But, really, it is our questions during our reading that make us want to read on and that give us the best chance of learning new information.

. . . Our questions begin from the moment we look at a book or an article. We wonder: What will this be about? What will I learn? The most important questions are those the *reader* asks.

. . . We even use our questions about unfamiliar words to help us as we read. Just by questioning a word, we often find clues that lead us to its meaning. (Show kids an example of a new or challenging term and how you make sense of it.)

. . . I found a very interesting text for us to read today. Take a look! Turn and talk about questions that pop immediately into your minds.

Teach/Model

- Show kids how you **question as you read.** Help them see that you ask and perhaps find answers to questions as you read. As you model, make your thinking explicit and show that by writing your own questions on Post-its you leave tracks of your thinking.

- Model how you **record and code an answer,** moving the Post-it to the part of the text where you find the answer.

- **Show kids how to use all sources** to answer questions. Even in sophisticated picture books, the author and illustrator work as a team to share the information a reader needs for understanding.

. . . As I read, I am going to share my questions and record them on Post-its.

. . . Just looking at the title, I already have a question. (Write the question on a Post-it and place it near the title.)

. . . As I read, I will continue to ask questions. Maybe I'll find some answers to my questions, and maybe not. We may not be able to answer all our questions, and that's okay. (Read part of the text and continue using Post-its to record your questions.)

. . . Turn and talk about questions you have.

. . . As I read, I am answering some of my earlier questions. We question as we read, and we note when we find an answer. When I find an answer, I'll jot it on the Post-it and code it with an *A* for *answer.* Then I'll leave the Post-it by the answer in the text. (As you find an answer to a previously asked question, jot it on the Post-it and move it to the part of the text that answers the question.)

. . . Notice that I sometimes use the pictures and other features to help me. Even asking the question—hearing myself say the question—helps me find the answer.

. . . Now you'll do the same. You will use Post-its to record your own questions as you read.

Guide/Support Practice

TEACHING MOVES

- Give kids Post-its and **have them read on,** noting their questions and any answers they find on their Post-its.

- Listen in and **provide support as needed.** Ask kids to share their thinking as they read. By having kids think aloud as you did, you can better coach them within the reading performance. Though most readers question as they read, some students may be less aware of their inner conversation.

TEACHING LANGUAGE

. . . I am going to give you Post-its. Use them to write your questions as you read. When you find an answer, write a few words to record the answer, and code the Post-it with an *A*.

. . . I will listen in on your reading and thinking, so if you have questions, I will be ready to answer them.

> **Teaching Tip**
>
> Personal questions are what propel readers on. Nonfiction satisfies our natural curiosity and desire to learn like no other genre. When readers awaken to the natural line of questions they develop as they read, their reading becomes not only more productive, but also more enjoyable.

Wrap Up

- After kids finish reading, have them **share their Post-its.**

- **Make a chart** to record students' questions and the answers they found in the text. This shows students how asking our own questions helps us identify new learning.

- Have students **keep their Post-its in their texts.** They will need them in the next session, when they consider unanswered questions.

- Supply Post-its so students can **continue questioning in their independent reading.**

> **Teaching Tip**
> Students need to read books they can sink their teeth into. For independent reading, consider nonfiction narratives like *The Wolf Girls* by Jane Yolen and Heidi Stemple, *Wilma Unlimited* by Kathleen Krull, and *Tigress* by Nick Dowson. Books like these inspire kids to ask authentic questions and search for answers.

. . . Let's turn and talk about our Post-its. Some of you may even have the same questions. We often have different questions because of our own background knowledge and experience.

. . . Let's make a chart of some of our questions and the answers we found in the text. Notice how our questions help us identify new learning. (Have kids share their questions and answers.)

Questioning

Questions	Answers

. . . Great job! It seems we have some questions we weren't able to answer. We will talk about any unanswered questions in our next session, so keep those Post-its in your texts.

. . . Now, you will want to keep questioning when you read in your independent books. Here are some extra Post-its. Keep questioning and looking for those answers!

ASSESS AND PLAN

Did students realize the value of questioning—how asking questions makes them more aware of new learning as they read?

Some students may be less aware of their own inner conversation and the questions that are a natural part of active reading. Provide additional modeling and confer with readers individually so they can think aloud as they read. This often strengthens their awareness and offers them the support they need to become more engaged.

Did students ask a variety of questions?

Check to make sure kids are asking questions that move beyond a literal meaning of the text—questions that begin with *why* or *how*. These small-group sessions provide an opportunity to review questioning stems: *Why . . . ? How . . . ? When . . . ? What . . . ?*

> *If readers are going to move toward independence, they need opportunities to think about their reading experiences and reflect on their strengths and challenges.* (Szymusiak and Sibberson, 2001)

Companion to . . .

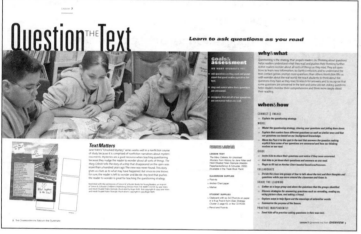

The Comprehension Toolkit
Lesson 7: Question the Text

Identify Unanswered Questions

This session builds on the previous one. Students identify the questions they asked that were not answered in the text.

TEXT MATTERS

We continue with the same text so readers see that although many of their questions were answered as they read on, some were not. We want kids to see that not all questions are answered as we read.

CONSIDERATIONS FOR PLANNING

While many questions are answered as readers read on, some are not. We want kids to see that they can continue to pursue answers in places other than one particular text. Authentic inquiry spurs readers on and often leads to more reading, more learning, and more satisfying reading and writing experiences.

Have on hand the *Questioning* anchor chart from the previous session.

Students will need their texts with Post-its from the previous session.

Students will need Post-its for this session if they haven't finished the text.

SESSION GOAL

We want students to:
■ recognize that not all of our questions are answered when we read.

Build Background, Word and Concept Knowledge

- **Review what students did** in the previous session.

- Use the anchor chart created in the previous session to **get kids thinking about their questions** and the answers they found.

TEACHING LANGUAGE

. . . Last time we met we learned how important it is to ask questions as we are reading. We found that as we read on, we answered many of our questions, but not all of them!

. . . Let's look at our anchor chart. Who wants to share a question we asked and the answer we found in the text?

. . . Today we are going to look back in our texts to look at the questions that were left unanswered and consider how we might find answers.

Teach/Model

TEACHING MOVES

- Find a place in the text **where you had a question that wasn't answered.** Model how you code the Post-it with *NA* to show that this question wasn't answered in the text.

- **Have students share their questions** that haven't been answered, even if you know they will find answers as they read on.

TEACHING LANGUAGE

. . . As I look back, I remember right here I had a question that wasn't answered in the text. I am going to code my Post-it with *NA* for *not answered*.

. . . As readers, we ask our questions as we read, and many of our questions are answered. We find the answers right in the text as we read on. But some of our questions may not be answered in the text.

. . . So let's consider questions you had that were not answered.

Guide/Support Practice

- Move among the students as they skim the text, rereading as necessary, to **find unanswered questions.**

- If kids haven't finished the text, have them read on, continuing to **record and code on Post-its.**

- Encourage students to **share aha! discoveries and answers.**

. . . Reread quickly, skimming the text to identify the Post-its with unanswered questions.

. . . If you didn't finish the text, read on. Continue writing your questions on Post-its and coding them: *A* if you find an answer, *NA* for no answer.

. . . I will be here to help you as needed.

Wrap Up

- After kids finish rereading (and reading on), have them share the Post-its on which they have written unanswered questions. **Collect their Post-its on an anchor chart.**

- **Briefly discuss how they might find answers.** You will go into these strategies in more depth in the next session.

. . . Let's share our unanswered questions. (Create an anchor chart to collect the unanswered questions.)

Our Unanswered Questions

. . . Great job! We learned how our questions are so important to us as readers. Some we answer immediately in the text, and others we realize aren't answered.

. . . The ones we are *very* curious about lead us to more opportunities to inquire, read, and talk to others who know more about the topic.

. . . As we study more about questioning as readers, we will explore ways to get our questions answered!

ASSESS AND PLAN

Did students question throughout the text?

Since questioning will be new for many students, keep note of how frequently they question. When you see very few questions, coach the student and invite the student to use Post-its in independent reading. You can use the Post-its in the independent text to gain more insight.

Did students use a variety of language stems in their questions?

Check to make sure students are asking questions that begin with *why* and *how*, as well as the more literal stems *what*, *who*, and *when*.

Did students miss answers to their questions as they read?

It might be helpful when this happens to actually help kids list their questions as they read, in a journal. By listing the questions, they can review their questions from time to time to see if they found an answer to one of them they might have missed.

Did some students really struggle with asking their own questions?

Consider finding a short piece of text and adding authentic questions in the margin that mirror what you want students to do themselves. This seems to be a helpful scaffold for some readers.

> *We need to support students in becoming more self-sustaining, thoughtful, independent readers and writers.*
> (Routman, 2003)

Companion to . . .

The Comprehension Toolkit
Lesson 8: Read to Discover Answers

Read with Your Questions in Mind

In *The Comprehension Toolkit* Lesson 8, students focus on asking questions to gain information, and they learn to use a variety of strategies to find answers. The three companion sessions for Lesson 8 break down this process. In this first session, students focus on strategies they can use to ask and answer their own questions as they read.

TEXT MATTERS

Questioning occurs as the result of reading interesting texts that invite authentic questions. We want to choose texts that will cause kids to puzzle over ideas and wonder as they read. Select a text that connects to your students' interests.

Articles like "Turn It Off" in the *Source Book of Short Text*, "Chocolate" in *Toolkit Texts: Grades 4–5*, and "Our Exciting Solar Neighborhood" and "Whose Feet Are Whose?" in *Toolkit Texts: Grades 2–3* provide enough information to stimulate kids' questions and yield some answers. Offering kids several articles to choose from works well. Make enough copies in case kids all choose the same article.

For independent reading, consider *Mailing May* by Michael O. Tunnell. This book keeps readers wondering and asking questions.

SESSION GOAL

We want students to:

- keep their questions in mind as they read in order to search for information that extends their learning.

CONSIDERATIONS FOR PLANNING

This session is designed to help kids see how we read to find answers to our questions. We want kids to see that when we keep our questions in mind, our reading deepens and our learning and understanding increase. We teach kids to use procedural strategies to make their reading and search for answers more efficient.

Be prepared to create two anchor charts.

Students will need copies of the *Questions/Answers/Strategies* chart.

Build Background, Word and Concept Knowledge

- We **engage kids** by offering interesting texts and topics. When readers are genuinely interested in a topic, authentic questions come naturally.

- One of the important things we want kids to learn is that **by being strategic, they increase their efficiency.** Readers sometimes use rereading as a strategy, but they do so in inefficient ways. Simply rereading without a purpose, question, or idea of what you are looking for is exhausting!

- **Introduce the word *strategy*.** *Strategy* means "a plan of action to achieve an overall aim." When readers are strategic, they are "planful" in their actions.

Teaching Tip

Some have suggested that if we read with a pencil in hand, we read more thoughtfully. The same might be said of reading with a question in mind. Our questions work to encourage us as we read, often providing just the right motivation to read on to gain answers.

. . . We have been investigating how useful questions are in our reading. As we read, we use what we know, but we also use our questions and the author's words and ideas to learn—we are information gatherers.

. . . When I am reading, sometimes I realize I haven't been paying attention. When that happens, I have a little talk with myself to get back on track. I double-back to where my mind wandered and, with a question in mind, I read again. That happens to all of us. When we keep questions in our mind, we find reading much more productive!

. . . Turn and talk about experiences you have had like that.

. . . As we'll discover, there are some useful strategies that help us answer our questions efficiently. A *strategy* is a plan or way of doing something. We will talk about some of the ways we can manage our questions and find answers for them.

Teach/Model

- Invite kids to think of all the possible strategies they can use for answering questions as they read. **Make an anchor chart to record strategies.**

- **Probe for and model these strategies** for answering questions:
  - Read on to find out.
  - Use clues from the text.
  - Use what we know—our background knowledge.

- **Introduce the *Questions/Answers/Strategy* chart.** Demonstrate how to read with questions in your mind and how to find the answers. Make your inner conversation explicit for kids.

. . . Let's brainstorm some ways we can get our questions answered—strategies we can use. We call them strategies because they are carefully selected plans. We'll make an anchor chart to record our ideas.

. . . Right! We found answers to some of our questions in the text as we read on in our last session. (Add kids' ideas to the chart and prompt for others as you talk about how to answer questions.)

Strategies for Answering Questions

- Read on—use text clues.
- Talk to a friend.
- Use background knowledge—your own or someone else's.

. . . Let's try using some of these strategies as we read today.

. . . Today we'll use another anchor chart. This time we will keep track of questions and the answers we find. We will also record how we use strategies to find the answers.

Questions	Answers	Strategies for Answering Questions

. . . I will keep track of the questions as we read. (Read the first part of the article or book you've selected. Stop and record as you read, using the anchor chart to show your thinking.)

Guide/Support Practice

TEACHING MOVES

- Review the anchor chart to **be sure kids understand what they are to do.**

- **Have students use a small version of the chart.** You can make copies of the form provided on page 44 of *The Comprehension Toolkit* Strategy Book 3: *Ask Questions* or have kids make their own *Questions/Answers/Strategies* charts.

- **Provide support as needed** by listening in on students' reading and recording.

TEACHING LANGUAGE

. . . Let's look at our anchor chart and review the strategies we used.

. . . Now I'm going to give you a small chart like our anchor chart. Jot your questions. When you find an answer, add it to the chart and write the strategy you used.

. . . I will listen in on your reading and thinking, so if you have questions, I will be ready to answer them.

Wrap Up

TEACHING MOVES

- After kids finish reading, have them **share their charts.**

- **Discuss the questions, answers, and strategies** they used, supporting kids with language that accurately captures what they did.

> **Teaching Tip**
> Help kids use the language of reading to notice and name what they do. When they use precise and consistent language, learning occurs much more quickly and transfers to new situations.

TEACHING LANGUAGE

. . . Let's look at what you wrote on your charts. Turn and talk about your questions, answers, and strategies. What do we want to add to our anchor chart?

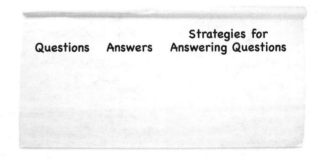

Questions	Answers	Strategies for Answering Questions

. . . You did a good job today! We will learn more about questioning when we meet again.

ASSESS AND PLAN

Were students able to label their strategies to get answers?
Helping kids articulate their thinking encourages them to become active learners who monitor their understanding as they read. While we encourage students to name and describe the thinking strategies they use, we remind them that we use strategies to further our understanding. It's not about parroting terms; instead, we check that students are using strategies and talking about their thinking in authentic ways.

> *In brief, the function of knowledge is to make one experience freely available to other experiences.*
> (Dewey, 1916)

Companion to . . .

The Comprehension Toolkit
Lesson 8: Read to Discover Answers

Session Goals

We want students to:
- keep their questions in mind as they read in order to search for information that extends their learning.
- understand that we arrive at answers using a variety of strategies, such as skimming and scanning.

Skim and Scan to Search for Answers

This session builds on the previous one. Students focus on strategies they can use to search for answers in a text. They learn to use the navigational strategies of skimming and scanning.

Text Matters

We want kids to navigate texts efficiently. For this session, select a text that provides reasons to use navigational strategies like skimming and scanning.

Graphic texts offer engaging opportunities for students because reading is seldom linear in them. Consider using "Stealing Freedom" in *Toolkit Texts: Grades 6–7* or "The Chocolate Belt" in *Toolkit Texts: Grades 4–5*. Both have maps, keys, and text readers must consider and navigate.

Selections like "Big Talkers" in the *Source Book of Short Text* and "Slithering Snakes" in *Toolkit Texts: Grades 2–3* may also suit your readers. These have features kids can use to search for information and answers to their questions.

Considerations for Planning

Learning how to skim and scan a text is an important, useful strategy kids will use throughout their lifetime. We want kids to learn ways to efficiently navigate a text. Texts that include visual and text features can be challenging, but when we model for students how they can skim, scan, and gain information from both visuals and text to answer their questions, they become more resourceful readers.

Have on hand the *Strategies for Answering Questions* anchor chart from the previous session.

Students will need Post-its for this session.

Build Background, Word and Concept Knowledge

- We want kids to learn that by developing text management strategies, they become better readers. Not only do they better understand the text and learn from it, they also enjoy reading more because they can access **strategies that make them more efficient.**

- Explain the concept of "navigating" text. **Introduce the terms** *skimming* **and** *scanning.*

- Have kids **think of times they have used skimming and scanning.** Some they might suggest:
  - looking in a list or a phone book
  - looking at a picture, illustration, or chart
  - looking at a map
  - looking for specific information

- **Add skimming and scanning** to the *Strategies* anchor chart.

. . . Today we will keep learning about how questions help us as readers. I want to teach you a very helpful strategy for reading text. It is really two strategies that are often used together to "navigate" text.

. . . When you think about a pilot, you think about someone flying a plane. But a pilot must also either have or be a "navigator" to be sure to stay on course. Readers are similar. They need ways to help them navigate texts that may sometimes feel a little complicated.

. . . We use two strategies or tools that work together and come in really handy, especially in nonfiction texts. They are called *skimming* and *scanning.*

. . . When we *skim* a text, we are trying to get a sense of what the text is about. We get the "big picture" when we skim. When we *scan* a text, we are often in search of key words or ideas. We are looking quickly to find something. The great thing about these two strategies is they work together as partners as we read.

. . . I bet you have used both skimming and scanning without knowing it! Turn and talk about when you might have used either of these strategies.

. . . Let's add skimming and scanning to our *Strategies for Answering Questions* chart from our last meeting.

> **Strategies for Answering Questions**
> - Read on—use text clues.
> - Talk to a friend.
> - Use background knowledge—your own or someone else's.
> - Use skimming and scanning

Teach/Model

■ In this session, we **invite kids to try skimming and scanning** as strategies for locating answers to their questions.

. . . I have selected a really interesting text for us to read. And, you know what, it will be much easier to read if we navigate it by skimming and scanning.

. . . Let's take a look. As you look at it, what questions do you immediately have? We'll use an anchor chart like we used before. (Jot kids' questions and your own on the chart.)

Questions	Answers	Strategies for Answering Questions

. . . Let's see if we can tackle some of these! Let's take the first one. Hmmm, I think we need to skim and scan to see where we might find the answer to our question. Try this on your copy. Turn and talk about what you are finding.

. . . Right here I found some words similar to those I used in my question. I was skimming and scanning quickly—reading the text and looking for words like those in my question. So I found this part that answers my question.

. . . Let's try one more question. (Demonstrate how you sometimes skim and scan by running your finger across the page.) Here are some words that answer my question. Let me read the question and the text. Now I've found the answer to my question. What do you think? Turn and talk.

Guide/Support Practice

- Kids may need more support. You may want them to **work in pairs** so they have not only your support, but also peer support.

- As an alternative or in addition to the Post-its, you can **have students use individual *Questions/Answers/Strategies* charts again.** Copy the form found on page 44 of *The Comprehension Toolkit* Strategy Book 3: *Ask Questions* or have kids make their own charts.

- **Let kids know** that you will support them as they need you, but **you want them to try it.**

. . . Now it's your turn. Let's look at the *Questions/Answers/Strategies* anchor chart and the questions we still want to answer. By the way, you may identify more questions as you read!

. . . Jot the question on a Post-it and put the Post-it where you find an answer. Remember how we coded? Draw a line under the question and put an *A* for the answer if and when you find it.

. . . If you get stuck, I will be here to help you, but I really want you to see how this works!

Wrap Up

- After kids finish reading, have them **share their Post-its or charts.**

- **Discuss** the questions, answers, and how the strategy of skimming and scanning worked.

. . . Let's look at what you did. Turn and talk about how you used skimming and scanning to help you locate answers.

. . . You likely still have some questions you couldn't answer because all our questions will almost never be answered in a single text. But I bet it helped to have a new tool!

Assess and Plan

Were kids able to use skimming and scanning effectively to find answers?

It is likely students will need additional practice. If you saw confusion, plan to sit side-by-side with individual students to offer more modeling and coached support.

As students read, check to see that they are:

- monitoring and leaving tracks of their thinking.
- noticing new learning from both text and features.
- stopping to ask questions and reading to answer them.

Curriculum is often thought of as a set of specific knowledge, skills, or books to be covered. I propose instead that we think of curriculum as a set of important conversations that we want students to engage in. (Applebee, 2001)

Companion to . . .

The Comprehension Toolkit
Lesson 8: Read to Discover Answers

Combine Knowledge and Text Information

This session builds on the previous one. Students focus on strategies they can use to find answers that aren't stated in the text: combining their background knowledge and text information, sharing and discussing background knowledge, and doing further research.

Text Matters

We want to show kids that our questions often lead us not only to read the text but also to combine our background knowledge with information in the text to infer answers. Sometimes we have to ask others or do further research to search for answers.

For this session we choose a text that has some ambiguity so students can see how readers answer questions by gathering clues from the text. Select a text on a topic that kids will have some background knowledge about and can research further if they have unanswered questions.

Short texts such as "The Japanese-American Internment" or "Navajo Code Talkers" in *Toolkit Texts: Grades 4–5*, "Flying High" in *Toolkit Texts: Grades 2–3*, and "The Super Ant" in the *Source Book of Short Text* provide enough information to stimulate kids to ask questions, infer, share and discuss background knowledge, and do further research.

Considerations for Planning

In this session, we support students in using a variety of strategies to search for answers that aren't stated in the text. At times, readers must combine their background knowledge and the information in the text to answer their questions. Sometimes they have to connect details and ideas from different parts of the text. Even then not all questions will be answered. We want kids to see that reading often leads us to further investigation. Our questions drive further research.

Students will need Post-its for this session.

Session Goal

We want students to:

■ understand that we arrive at answers using a variety of strategies, such as inferring, sharing and discussing background knowledge, and doing further research.

Build Background, Word and Concept Knowledge

- We want kids to learn that **a clear-cut answer may not appear in the text.**

- We also want kids to learn **we sometimes figure out the answer by combining** our background knowledge with information in the text.

> **Teaching Tip**
>
> We want to be sure students understand that they must amass evidence to support an answer. We show them how to read on and consider additional information.

. . . We have been learning so much about questioning and how important our questions are in reading.

. . . Today we will explore another way we can find answers to the questions that arise before, during, and even after our reading.

. . . Readers sometimes have to enter into a partnership with the author. Our answers sometimes come by combining what we know—our background knowledge—with information in the text.

. . . Let's try it!

Teach/Model

■ **We invite kids to explore** how their own background knowledge can help them answer their questions.

■ By having kids **think about their background knowledge** prior to reading, we make sure it is ready to access.

■ **Preview** any unfamiliar vocabulary.

■ **Begin a chart** to record kids' background knowledge, questions, and answers.

■ **Discuss ways students could research** to find answers to lingering questions: looking in other books, searching online, asking a librarian for help, etc.

. . . I have selected a text for us to read. You all are likely to know a little about the topic already. Here's the topic . . . Turn and talk about what you think you know about . . . .

. . . Let's create an anchor chart to show what we think we know about . . . . (Begin recording in the first column of the anchor chart.)

What We Think We Know About (Topic)	Questions We Have About (Topic)	Answers Using BK and Text Clues

. . . Here's a word that may be new to you. Let's talk about what it means.

. . . As you skim and scan the text, what questions come to mind? Turn and talk about those. Let's add the questions we have to our chart.

. . . Now I will read a bit of the text to show how we tap both our own ideas and the information in the text to answer our questions. (Use one of your own questions to model.)

. . . Turn and talk about what you are noticing. Yes! We were able to answer one of our questions by simply discussing our background knowledge. (Record the answer on the chart.)

. . . Let's try another one. (Use a question that isn't answered by the text or kids' background knowledge.) Here's a question that we don't seem to be able to answer. We call it a *lingering* question. Remember, we can't always answer all our questions.

Guide/Support Practice

- Have kids use Post-its to **mark places in the text where they find clues** that help them figure out answers to their questions.

- **Assure students** they may continue coming up with additional questions as they read.

. . . As you read to answer one of our questions, or if you think of a new question, consider how what you know may help you figure out the answer.

. . . Let's keep reading to see if we can answer other questions . . . . Yes! Here's some information that helps to answer our question about . . . .

. . . Let's read on and try to find support in the text for our answer. When you think you have found some information that answers the question, put the answer on a Post-it right where you found the information.

. . . If we can't answer every question, that's okay! We can continue to keep our questions in mind as we read.

Wrap Up

- **Review the strategies** of reading on for more information and discussing background knowledge to answer a question.

- Some questions aren't answered. Be sure to remind kids that our **lingering questions are great opportunities** for further research.

. . . Notice what we did. We talked about our background knowledge to answer a question. And we read on for more information so we could answer our questions.

. . . Who can show us an example and explain how you used information from the text or your BK (background knowledge) to answer it? Or maybe you used both! (Add answers to the anchor chart.)

. . . We found answers to most of our questions, but we left a few unanswered. When we have unanswered questions we are really curious about, we get new opportunities to read and do some research!

ASSESS AND PLAN

Did kids' understanding of questioning and searching for answers grow over the three sessions? Did they become more articulate and confident learners?

Additional sessions will continue to help kids grow more aware of their questions and to use them productively to learn from their reading. Continue to find opportunities for students to practice the strategies of skimming and scanning.

As students read, check to see that they continue to use strategies introduced previously:

- stop, think, react, and sometimes ask a question.
- pay attention to the features to help answer a question.
- read with a question in mind to try to answer it.
- understand that they can read on, use their background knowledge, and talk to someone to answer a question.

Ask Questions to Understand Big Ideas

In *The Comprehension Toolkit* Lesson 9, students wonder and ask questions about the text to understand big ideas in a read-aloud biography.

Companion to . . .

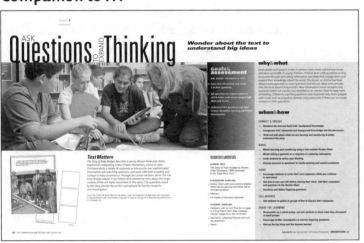

The Comprehension Toolkit
Lesson 9: Ask Questions to
Expand Thinking

The two sessions supporting Lesson 9 offer students the opportunity to practice asking questions to expand their thinking about information and ideas in another text. In this first session, students focus on asking questions to better understand information and ideas in the text.

TEXT MATTERS

For this session we want to select a text that will lead to questions as well as refine and expand kids' knowledge of the world.

Texts that feature well-known people and events engage kids in questioning and refining their background knowledge. Biographies like *Martin's Big Words* by Doreen Rappaport, *Rosa* by Nikki Giovanni, or *Snowflake Bentley* by Jacqueline Briggs Martin inspire kids to ask questions and think about big ideas. You can read part of the book in this session and invite kids to explore further in the next session or in their independent reading.

Short texts like "Clouds" and "Penguins in Motion" in *Toolkit Texts: Grades 2–3* also work well for this session. They expand kids' thinking about familiar phenomena.

CONSIDERATIONS FOR PLANNING

When we connect students to topics that involve important people and events, we offer them reading experiences that matter. Kids construct their own knowledge, but we must provide a rich environment so this can occur. Complex issues and ideas engage kids. We use that engagement to show that tangling with important ideas and issues can be enormously satisfying!

Kids will need Post-its for this session.

SESSION GOALS

We want students to:
- learn new information and relate it to their questions.
- ask questions to resolve confusion and to better understand complicated ideas and issues.

Build Background, Word and Concept Knowledge

- We want kids to learn that **questioning and wondering are tools** we use to think about and learn from our reading.

- **Preview or review any pertinent vocabulary** that will facilitate students' comprehension.

Teaching Tip

We want to be sure to incorporate what kids tell us about their background knowledge into our discussion. When we weave in kids' thoughtful comments, they understand how helpful their knowledge and experiences are in preparing to read a new text.

. . . We have learned so much lately about how our questions and what we wonder about make our reading more enjoyable and help us learn.

. . . We know that thinking about our background knowledge is important when we read, and we use it as a springboard to get us ready to read.

. . . Today we will be reading about a topic you already know a little about. As readers, what we discover is that the more we read, the more we add to our knowledge.

. . . Let's talk about a few words you will need to know . . .

Teach/Model

- We connect kids to texts that are interesting and address thoughtful, substantive issues. **Introduce the text** you have selected and ask kids to share their background knowledge about the topic.

- In this session, we want kids to think about the important ideas. But we also want them to notice that as they ask questions and wonder, **they may have to "work out their thinking"** to understand sophisticated ideas and issues.

- Be sure to **model how you resolve confusion as you read** by monitoring your understanding, rereading, and thinking about meaning. If answers to your questions are uncovered in the text, point that out so kids continue to see that reading is all about thinking, learning, and questioning.

- Demonstrate how you **ask a question and then keep reading,** uncovering the answer in subsequent text.

. . . I have selected a text that will make us *think* today. It's about . . . Turn and talk about what you already know about . . .

. . . Some of you already know something about . . . . But today as you read, you are going to learn even more. As you read, you are likely to have questions that surface and ideas that you wonder about.

. . . I'm going to think out loud as I read so you can see what happens as I learn new information. I'll record my thinking on this anchor chart as I read. Watch to see what you notice. (Begin reading and recording your own learning and questions.)

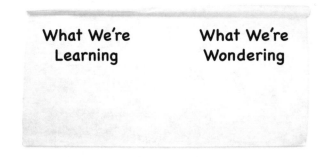

. . . Wow! Look at this. I didn't know . . . That's something I'm going to write on our chart. I'll write down just enough to help me remember. Turn and talk about what you're thinking.

. . . (Read on.) I think I will stop here and reread. I'm not quite clear on this part. (Reread.) This causes me to wonder . . . . I'll write that on our chart.

. . . And here I've answered my own question. I'll write the information down and put a small check next to the question to show I've found information that answers it.

. . . Now I want you to try it.

Guide/Support Practice

TEACHING MOVES

- Support kids as they **read and record on Post-its.** Prompt kids as necessary.
  - What did you learn?
  - What are you wondering?

TEACHING LANGUAGE

. . . It's your turn to read. Use Post-its to record and code your thinking, Put an *L* on the information you learn and a *Q* on your questions.

. . . I will be around to help you.

Wrap Up

- **Add kids' ideas to the *What We're Learning* column on the chart** and list their questions under *What We're Wondering*. As you do, talk about what questions are actually answered in the text. It is likely that some won't be.

- **Note any unanswered questions on the chart.** In the following session, you'll have an opportunity to invite kids to see those lingering questions as opportunities for continued reading and learning.

. . . Let's talk about what you are learning and wondering. Turn and talk about what you wrote.

. . . Let's add to our chart of what we are learning and wondering. (Have kids share their Post-its and record on the chart.)

What We're Learning	What We're Wondering

. . . I'm curious. Did anyone find a place where asking a question actually clarified your thinking and cleared up some confusion?

. . . And did anyone find that you answered a question as you kept reading?

. . . Interesting, isn't it, how reading is all about learning and questioning and finding answers to our questions.

. . . Sometimes we have a question and don't find an answer in the text. We call these *lingering* questions. They are often especially thoughtful questions.

. . . Are there any lingering questions on our chart? We can come back to them in our next session.

ASSESS AND PLAN

Were students able to use questioning to gain understanding and resolve confusion and misconceptions as they read?

Students sometimes need extra support and modeling to understand how their thinking evolves during reading. Confer with students individually to provide any extra support they need to see the connection between their questions and understanding.

Did students have lingering questions?

If students have finished the text and have lingering questions, consider selecting another text that will provide for continued exploration and learning in the next session. Students' lingering questions may launch substantive discussions about ideas and issues raised in the picture books suggested in Text Matters. For instance, *Rosa* and *Martin's Big Words* will prompt questions about issues such as injustice, racism, and prejudice, as well as historical questions about the civil rights movement and the important roles Martin Luther King, Jr., and Rosa Parks (among others) played in the struggle for equality.

> *We have to show how we as proficient adult learners notice and develop questions, how we search out and evaluate information, and how we put new knowledge to work and share it with others.*
> (Harvey and Daniels, 2009)

Companion to . . .

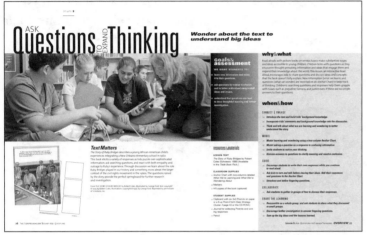

The Comprehension Toolkit
Lesson 9: Ask Questions to Expand Thinking

Session Goal

We want students to:
- understand that questions can lead to more thoughtful learning and further investigation.

Use Questions to Increase Learning

This session builds on the previous one. Students use their questions to increase their learning and plan further investigation.

Text Matters

Continue with the text from the previous session, or introduce another text that offers kids lots to think about. Longer texts, such as *Rosa* by Nikki Giovanni, may require more than one session, but they are worth reading because they raise many questions, extend learning, and capture student interest.

Considerations for Planning

In this session, we continue asking questions as a way to extend kids' learning. We offer kids the opportunity to see their lingering questions as a source for inquiry and new learning.

Have on hand the *What We're Learning/What We're Wondering* anchor chart from the previous session.

Students will need Post-its for this session.

Build Background, Word and Concept Knowledge

■ We want kids to see that not all questions are answered. We explain how those ***lingering questions* offer us great opportunities** for further research and learning.

. . . Questions! Questions! Questions! We have talked a lot about how useful they are to us as readers.

. . . Today we will continue to explore what we learn and how we question.

. . . Have any of you experienced a time when you just kept thinking about a particular question? That often happens when we encounter a question that just doesn't go away. It *lingers*. We call those questions *lingering questions*. They push us to think further and surface big ideas or issues.

Teach/Model

- Have kids **look back at the anchor chart** from the previous session. Point out the connections between the learning and the questions. Focus students' attention on the lingering questions.

- **If a new text is being used,** introduce it and preview any unfamiliar vocabulary.

. . . Today we will extend our learning about the role of questions in our reading. We'll keep reading in our book. (If a new text is being used, introduce it in the same way the previous text was introduced.)

. . . You remember when we last met, we recorded our learning on our anchor chart, and we also charted our questions. We found many of our questions were answered as we read on in the text. Let's look back at our anchor chart to see if that happened.

What We're Learning	What We're Wondering

. . . Turn and talk about what you notice. I recall that we put a small check by the questions we found answers for. What are some of your lingering questions, those that aren't answered yet?

. . . As you read on, let's see if any of these lingering questions are resolved. Or maybe we will figure out "answers" to these questions on our own. The text doesn't always "answer" our questions, but sometimes we can work out the answers ourselves.

Guide/Support Practice

- You might encourage kids to skim and scan the text to **see if they can answer any of their lingering questions.**

- **Explain to them how to home in** on specific parts of the text.

. . . Continue to use Post-its to record and code your thinking.

. . . I will be around to help you.

Wrap Up

- As you **add kids' learning and questions** to the chart, talk about what questions are actually answered in the text. It is likely that some won't be.

- Invite kids to **see lingering questions as opportunities** for continued reading and learning.

. . . Let's hear what today's reading brought you! What shall we add to our chart? Turn and talk about what you jotted on Post-its.

What We're Learning	What We're Wondering

. . . Let's record some of your new learning and questions. Thinking through the text and reflecting on the interesting questions you asked helped you surface some of the big ideas in this text.

. . . I'm noticing that some of our questions still aren't answered. Who remembers what we call those questions? Right! We call them *lingering* questions. They offer us great opportunities for further research, as well as discussions and conversations that extend our thinking.

. . . Who has a question that really intrigues you and that you would like to investigate?

. . . What is something important that you learned today? Who would like to share?

ASSESS AND PLAN

Do kids seem intrigued by ideas in the text and their unanswered questions?

Tolerating ambiguity is often difficult for young readers. They love to wrap up their reading and make it neat and tidy! However, it is just as important for kids to learn how reading pushes us forward as readers and thinkers. This session sets that idea in motion. One way to help kids become more curious, engaged readers is to help them turn their lingering questions into manageable research questions. Questions can be addressed and perhaps resolved through discussion and conversation. Or kids may come up with their own original responses to questions that aren't easily answered.

Reading Conference
Ask Questions

After this unit, you want to know that students are asking questions as they read and consciously reading to discover answers, so your conference should help the student think about the questions he or she has and keep them in mind while reading.

1. **Invite the student to choose a passage to read aloud. Explain that you will expect him or her to stop and ask a question about the text while reading.**
   - Choose a part of your text and read it to me.
   - Tell me what this is about.
   - *(If the student doesn't stop and question on his or her own)* What question(s) do you have about what you are reading right now?

2. **Focus on the questions the student asked and tried to answer while reading.**
   - Share some of the questions you have about what you have read.
   - Show a place where you got a question answered.
   - Share a question that did not get answered.
   - Show me a place where it was hard to understand what you were reading. How can asking a question help if you are confused?

3. **Ask the student to continue reading, this time with a question in mind.**
   - What question(s) do you have about this topic (or text) right now?
   - What are some ways you could find the answer?

   - Did you learn anything new? What do you wonder about that new information?
   - Show me how you might skim and scan to find an answer to your question.

Reading Conference Recording Form: Ask Questions	
Name _____ Date _____	
Book title _____	
GOAL	EVIDENCE
The student . . .	This student . . .
1. Understands and questions the text • Tells what the text is about and asks questions about it	
2. Asks questions and tries to answer them • Stops and asks a question to clarify meaning, to clear up confusion, or to express curiosity • Notices when his or her questions are answered • Recognizes that not all questions are answered when reading	
3. Reads with a question in mind and uses a variety of strategies to answer the question • Skims and scans to find answers • Reads on • Talks about it	

©2010 by Stephanie Harvey, Anne Goudvis, and Judy Wallis. From *Comprehension Intervention: Small-Group Lessons for The Comprehension Toolkit.* Portsmouth, NH: Heinemann. This page may be copied for classroom use only.

Conference Recording Form for "Ask Questions," located in "Resources" section.

Language students may use to demonstrate that they are asking questions

- I wonder . . .
- Why . . .
- How come . . .
- What . . . Where . . . When . . . Why . . .
- Huh? What's going on here?
- My big question is . . .

Follow-Ups

If the student has difficulty with any of the primary goals in this unit, prompts like the following may be helpful during independent work in subsequent units.

- What do you wonder about what you just read?
- Did you remember to stop and ask questions?
- Did you find an answer to your question?
- Did you keep your question in mind as you read?
- Did you have questions about information that was new to you?
- Do you have some strategies to get your questions answered?
- Were you ever confused? How did you fix that?

Infer Meaning

Inferring is the bedrock of understanding. Inferring involves drawing a conclusion or making an interpretation that is not explicitly stated in the text. Typically, skillful writers do not spill information onto the page all at once for everyone to see. They leak information slowly, one idea at a time, inviting the reader to make reasonable inferences. Inferential thinking allows readers to make predictions, surface themes, and draw conclusions.

Readers also visualize to infer meaning. When readers visualize, they create pictures in their minds of what the text tells them. In nonfiction reading, as one of our students characterized it, those pictures look more like a slide show or a newscast than a movie.

Active nonfiction readers get a freeze-frame in their minds of a spewing volcano and then suddenly burst with dozens of questions and reactions. Often, answers to these questions must be inferred. When reading nonfiction, readers may have to crack open language word by word to infer the meaning of unfamiliar vocabulary and concepts.

> *When students hear [and read] unfamiliar words to describe concepts they are familiar with and care about, they become curious about the world of words.* (Graves and Watts-Taffe, 2002)

Companion to . . .

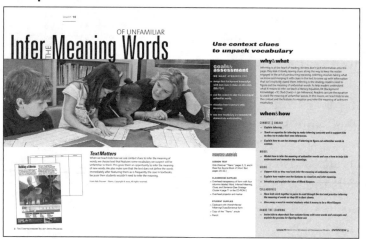

The Comprehension Toolkit
Lesson 10: Infer the Meaning of Unfamiliar Words

Use Context to Infer Word Meanings

In *The Comprehension Toolkit* Lesson 10, students infer the meaning of unfamiliar words in a read-aloud article. Then they demonstrate understanding by using the new vocabulary. The two companion sessions for Lesson 10 offer kids more practice with this process. In this first session, they review the inferring equation (TC + BK = I) and use context clues to infer the meanings of unfamiliar words in a new text.

TEXT MATTERS

For this session we want to choose a short text that offers kids the opportunity to explore a topic that includes content vocabulary.

Selections like "Wings in the Water" in *Toolkit Texts: Grades 2–3*, "Living at the Bottom of the World" in *Toolkit Texts: Grades 4–5*, and "The Money Game" or "Riding the Rails" in the *Source Book of Short Text* may suit your readers. These have content vocabulary and text clues kids can use to infer the meanings of unfamiliar words.

CONSIDERATIONS FOR PLANNING

In this session, we show kids that unfamiliar words are often accessible when we investigate the clues in the word's context.

We teach kids the inferring equation, which offers them a shorthand way to remember that when we find a gap in the text's meaning, we combine text clues with our own background knowledge and experience to fill the gap. Here is the inferring equation. We tell kids that it is similar to a math equation, like 2 + 2 = 4.

$$TC + BK = I$$
(**T**ext **C**lues + **B**ackground **K**nowledge = **I**nference)

Students will need Post-its for this session.

SESSION GOALS

We want students to:

- merge their background knowledge with text clues to make an inference (TC + BK = I).
- use context to infer meaning of unfamiliar words.

Build Background, Word and Concept Knowledge

TEACHING MOVES

- **Introduce the term** *inferring*.

- **Introduce the inferring equation:**
  TC + BK = I. Also write it out: *Text Clues plus Background Knowledge equals Inference.*

- **Help kids use the inferring equation** to figure out what it means to be a *word sleuth*.

- We want to help kids see that inferring is at the heart of reading. We encourage them to **be on the lookout for ways to make meaning.**

> **Teaching Tip**
>
> An exciting aspect of word consciousness is that it often leads kids to a dictionary or glossary to confirm meaning and make new words their own. When this happens, encourage kids to investigate and use and share what they learn.

TEACHING LANGUAGE

. . . Today we are going to learn about something very important for readers: *inferring.*

. . . You've heard about context clues, right? We use them to figure out an unfamiliar word as we read. We use clues from words and ideas surrounding the word we don't know to figure it out. That's *inferring*. When we read, we have to become word sleuths and use text clues and our background knowledge to solve the mystery of what words mean.

. . . I just used the word *sleuth*. Let's see how we can figure out what the word *sleuth* means. Here's my sentence. (Write it where kids can see it.)

> When we read, we have to become word <u>sleuths</u> and use text clues and our background knowledge to solve the mystery of what words mean.

. . . We can use an equation to help us infer. It's just like a math equation, like 2 + 2 = 4. (Write and explain the inferring equation.)

$$TC + BK = I$$
<u>T</u>ext <u>C</u>lues plus <u>B</u>ackground <u>K</u>nowledge
equals <u>I</u>nference

. . . Let's use the equation to infer the meaning of *sleuth*. (Scaffold students in getting to the idea that a sleuth investigates like a detective.)

> TC: clues, solve, mysteries
> BK: I know <u>detectives</u> use clues to solve mysteries.
> I: I can infer that the word <u>sleuth</u> means a kind of detective!

. . . So a *sleuth* must be someone who solves mysteries. And a "word sleuth" is someone who solves word mysteries, like a word detective. That's what we're doing today!

Teach/Model

- **Introduce the text.** Explain that you are going to think about unfamiliar words and make inferences about their meanings as you read.

- **Spend sufficient time modeling** to ensure students' success during guided practice.

- **Model practices to use** when they read independently.

. . . We are going to explore how we infer and use our background knowledge to help us figure out the meaning of unfamiliar words as we read.

. . . I selected a text I think you will like and one that will give us lots of opportunities to use our background knowledge and experiences to crack open the meaning of, or figure out, some interesting new words.

. . . Let me show you how this works. Listen while I read and think about the meaning of words that I am unfamiliar with.

. . . When I make an inference about a word while I am reading, I am going to write what I infer the word means on a Post-it and place it right in the text beside the word. Watch me write and then code with an *I* for *infer.* (Demonstrate how you record your inference about the word's meaning.)

. . . Turn and talk about what you saw me doing.

. . . Would someone share? Great! You are so right. You saw me pause when I was reading and note that I didn't know the word. Then I used my background knowledge and experience, which was . . . and the text clues, which were . . . . And I recorded my inference with an *I* on a Post-it!

. . . Let's read on a little more. (When you have offered several examples, turn the reading over to the students.)

Guide/Support Practice

- **Have students read on** and record their inferences on Post-its.

- **Move among the students,** listening in on their reading and supporting them as necessary.

. . . Now it's your turn. I will come around to hear you read and to see what you are inferring about unfamiliar words.

Wrap Up

TEACHING MOVES

- Debriefing what students did is critical. It offers a time to **share any observations you made** about their smart thinking and the way they used inferring to figure out the meaning of unfamiliar words.

- **Have kids share** some of their Post-its and the inferences they made.

- **Have students save their Post-its** or make a list of new words for the next session.

TEACHING LANGUAGE

. . . So, what did you notice as you read? Right! You found some places where you were unsure of the meaning of a word and you used your own background knowledge and experience to help you figure it out—you inferred!

. . . You combined your BK with clues from the text (TC) to make an inference!

. . . Let's share a few examples. Look back in your text for places you put a Post-it. Turn and talk with your neighbor, sharing your inferences.

. . . Save your Post-its for our next session.

Assess and Plan

Did students identify text clues with ease and use them to infer the meanings of unknown words?

Students may need additional models to understand how to read around an unfamiliar word and identify context clues. Consider creating a visual model of the inferring equation. Select a paragraph that has an unknown word and give each student a copy. Have kids highlight and cut out (or write on a Post-it) words in the text that give clues about the unknown word. Have them record their background knowledge on Post-its. Then have them group the text clues and Post-its to illustrate the equation: TC + BK = I. Have them write their inference (the meaning of the unknown word) to complete the visual model.

Use New Vocabulary

This session builds on the previous one. Students use new vocabulary to demonstrate their understanding of the text.

TEXT MATTERS

We want to help kids see that when they encounter a new word, they can "capture" it and make that unfamiliar word one they own.

We have kids use the same text and investigate more closely the new words they identified in the previous session.

CONSIDERATIONS FOR PLANNING

We continue to show kids that inferring the meaning of unknown words from context is an important strategy to know and use throughout their lives. In this session, we show them how they can make a new word their own by investigating how they infer the meaning and then using the word in a sentence.

We use the vocabulary chart from page 71 of *The Comprehension Toolkit* Strategy Book 4: *Infer Meaning*, to show kids how to infer and then transfer meaning so the words become their own. You can copy the form provided in *The Comprehension Toolkit* or make the chart as shown in Teach/Model.

Students will need their new words from the previous session.

Students will need individual copies of the vocabulary chart used in this session.

Companion to . . .

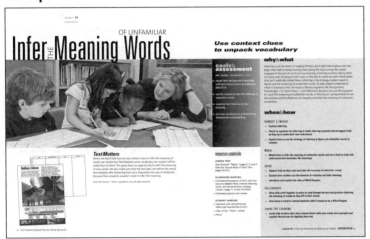

The Comprehension Toolkit
Lesson 10: Infer the Meaning
of Unfamiliar Words

SESSION GOAL

We want students to:

- use new vocabulary in a sentence to demonstrate understanding.

Build Background, Word and Concept Knowledge

- We want to help kids understand that by **using the new word in a sentence** of their own, they increase their chance of learning the word.

- **Review the inferring equation** to remind students how they infer the meaning of a new word.

. . . Today we are going to look back at the words we identified as unfamiliar the last time we read.

. . . Remember, we talked about how we could use the inferring equation to figure out the meaning of new words.

$$TC + BK = I$$

. . . I want to show you a way to investigate the text clues and also how to make the new words you find your own.

Teach/Model

- **Have kids recall new words** and how they inferred meaning.

- **If kids seem confused** about using the inferring equation, offer a quick model. Making sure they understand the equation and how it works is essential for success in this session.

- **Model how to use the vocabulary chart** to record a new word, its inferred meaning, clues in the text, and a sentence that uses the word in a way that demonstrates understanding.

- **Give students individual charts** to use for their own words from the previous session.

. . . Let's look at the words you identified last time we met together.

. . . Turn and talk about the unfamiliar words you found and how you inferred their meaning. Tell how you used the inferring equation.

. . . Let's make a chart to help us investigate not only how we inferred through text clues, but also how we create a sentence with the word that demonstrates its meaning.

Word	Inferred Meaning	Clues	Sentence
thermal	warm	"weather very cold" "special clothing"	It was so cold, they had to wear thermal underwear to stay warm.

. . . I am going to give you charts that look just like this one. Go back through the text and complete the chart with your own words.

Guide/Support Practice

TEACHING MOVES

- **Observe the kids working in pairs** to be sure they understand their task.

- **Scaffold as necessary** by showing kids how to read around the word to infer meaning from the text clues.

TEACHING LANGUAGE

. . . Let's try one out together. Work in pairs with one of your words. I'll help you if you need me.

. . . Now it's your turn. I will come around to see how you're doing. One suggestion . . . you may need to reread the text! Good readers know that rereading often helps them notice something they hadn't noticed before.

Wrap Up

TEACHING MOVES

- **Have kids share** their charts. Add examples to the group chart.

- Be sure to notice that kids' sentences actually **demonstrate they understand the meaning.** Some sentences will use the word, but students' understanding of the meaning will not be obvious from the sentence.

TEACHING LANGUAGE

. . . How did it go?

. . . Let's take a look at your charts. Turn and talk and then we'll add a few to our group chart.

. . . Great work! You'll find that by being strategic and *sleuthing* through the text, you'll infer the meaning of words and add them to your own vocabulary.

Assess and Plan

Did students use the chart with ease or demonstrate confusion?
Giving kids an additional copy of the vocabulary chart to use on their own in independent reading is a great way to offer more practice. Consider conferring with kids about their chart during independent reading time.

As kids create their charts, check to make sure they:

- understand how to use the context (by rereading and reading on) to infer the meanings of unfamiliar words.
- create sentences that clearly demonstrate their understanding of the newly learned word.

> *Activating relevant back-ground knowledge is a critical component of quality teach-ing. Importantly, it's not something that's done only at the outset of a unit or lesson.* (Fisher and Frey, 2009)

Companion to . . .

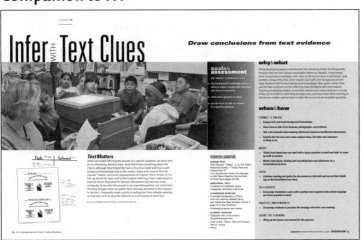

The Comprehension Toolkit
Lesson 11: Infer with Text Clues

SESSION GOALS

We want students to:

- read with a question in mind.
- gather facts to infer an answer to a specific question.

Gather Text Evidence

In *The Comprehension Toolkit* Lesson 11, students learn to draw conclu-sions from text evidence by reading with an overarching question in mind, gathering relevant facts from the text, and using the facts to make inferences that help them answer the question. The two companion sessions for Lesson 11 break down this process. In this first session, kids focus on an overarching question and gather relevant facts from the text as they read.

TEXT MATTERS

We want to select a text on a topic about which kids have some background knowledge. When kids already know something about the topic, their knowledge may include both accurate and inaccurate information.

"Firefighting through the Ages" in *Toolkit Texts: Grades 4–5* or "On the Move" and "Animal Ears" in *Toolkit Texts: Grades 2–3* lend themselves to reading with an overarching question in mind and gathering relevant infor-mation from the text and features.

For independent reading, consider books like *A Walk in the Rain Forest* by Rebecca Johnson. Most kids know something about rain forests and are eager to gather more information about overarching questions such as what they are, what's happening to them, and how they can be preserved.

CONSIDERATIONS FOR PLANNING

In this session, we ask an overarching question to help kids gather rele-vant facts from the text as they read to answer the question. In the next session, they will make inferences from the facts they have gathered and draw conclusions to answer the question. The text you select will have to lend itself to a focus question that can be asked before reading. Then kids will read to find information that answers the question.

Students will need Post-its for this session.

Build Background, Word and Concept Knowledge

- We want kids to understand that they will be reading with an authentic question in their mind, and **that question will influence how they read and the information they gather.**

- **Review with kids what a *fact* is.**

- Review the inferring equation. In previous sessions, students inferred the meanings of words from their context. In this session, **they will gather facts and infer to answer a question.**

. . . As we investigate a topic in our reading today, we will start by asking an important question about the topic. Then, as we read, we will gather facts to help us answer our question.

. . . What is a *fact*? Right! A fact is accurate information that is "right there" in the text.

. . . Remember, we use information or evidence from the text—text clues—and merge this information with our background knowledge to make an inference. TC + BK = I. That's the inferring equation.

. . . Keep all that in mind as we read today!

Teach/Model

- **Introduce the text** and invite kids to share their background knowledge about the topic.

- **Preview any vocabulary words** that may be unfamiliar, encouraging kids to infer their meaning from the context.

- We want kids to see that **when we gather facts, we use those to infer** because we are really "building a case" for our inference.

- **Develop a focus question** that kids can use to focus their attention and gather information as they read.

- As you begin reading, demonstrate how you **notice relevant facts and record them** on an anchor chart.

```
                    QUESTION
     Facts
```

. . . Let's look at the text I've brought. As you preview it, what do you know about the topic?

. . . Great! Your background knowledge—all the information you mentioned—will help you as you read.

. . . Let's quickly preview a few vocabulary words you'll need to know . . . .

. . . As I think about this topic, I can't help but wonder . . . (Develop an overarching focus question that fits the text. For example: What could we learn about firefighting from the past? What do animals do with their ears? What can we do to preserve the rain forest?)

. . . Let's see how this works. I am going to make an anchor chart for recording. I'll put our focus question at the top. That's the question we will be thinking about, or focusing on, as we read. We'll record the facts we find that relate to our question.

. . . Let me read the first page. Here's an interesting fact that relates to our question . . . . I'll record that on our chart.

. . . As I read, I am keeping our question in mind. (Read on.) Hmmm . . . here's another fact. But notice how this one *doesn't* help to answer our question.

. . . Turn and talk about a fact you found that helps to answer our question. Notice you merged the information with your BK to answer the question.

. . . Does everyone see how this works?

Guide/Support Practice

TEACHING MOVES

- **Give kids Post-its to record relevant facts** they find as they read on. Tell them to code their Post-its with an *F* when they record a *fact*.

- Before moving around to **listen to kids read,** observe them. By observing, we learn so much about their understanding of the task and their confidence in their performance.

TEACHING LANGUAGE

. . . Now it's your turn. I am going to give you some Post-its to use as you read on. When you find a relevant fact in the text, note it on a Post-it and code it with an *F* for *fact*.

. . . Remember to keep the question in mind as you read!

. . . I will be around to listen and help.

Wrap Up

TEACHING MOVES

- **Have kids share** some of their Post-its.

- Have kids select facts to **add to the chart.**

- **Kids will need their text with Post-its** for the next session.

TEACHING LANGUAGE

. . . Take a minute to turn and talk about what you learned and what you inferred.

. . . Let's see what we can add to our chart.

. . . Great thinking today! Next time we meet, we will continue thinking about this text and our focus question.

ASSESS AND PLAN

Did kids use the focus question to select relevant facts?

If selecting facts that relate to the big question challenges kids, consider creating a chart with the focus question in the middle. Have kids "test" their fact against the question before placing it on the chart as a fact that helps answer the question.

Make sure students are using the strategies from previous sessions as tools for understanding:

- listening to the inner voice
- paying attention to features
- connecting to background knowledge
- asking questions to gain information
- using the inferring equation to construct meaning

> *When readers infer, they create a meaning that is not explicitly stated in the text. The process implies that they actively search for or become aware of implicit meaning.* (Keene, 2008)

Draw and Support Conclusions

This session builds on the previous one. Students use the facts they have gathered from the text to make reasonable inferences and draw a conclusion about the focus question.

Companion to . . .

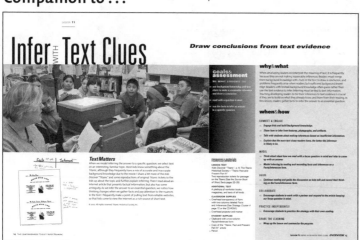

The Comprehension Toolkit
Lesson 11: Infer with Text Clues

TEXT MATTERS

Continue with the text used in the previous session.

CONSIDERATIONS FOR PLANNING

In this session, we help kids see how they use their background knowledge and the text clues (facts) they have gathered to make solid inferences. This session offers one more opportunity to show kids that the reading they do helps build background knowledge they will use in the future. We show students how the facts they've gathered can be combined with their background knowledge to infer answers to questions.

Have on hand the anchor chart from the previous session.

Students will need their text with Post-its from the previous session.

Students will need Post-its for this session.

SESSION GOALS

We want students to:

- use background knowledge and text clues to make a reasonable inference and draw a conclusion.
- read with a question in mind.
- use the facts to infer an answer to a specific question.

Build Background, Word and Concept Knowledge

TEACHING MOVES

- **Review students' understanding** of inferring, background knowledge, and facts.

TEACHING LANGUAGE

. . . Let's do what we do when we infer; let's activate our background knowledge *about* inferring! (Have kids share what they are learning about inferring, including the equation.)

. . . Today we are going to use the facts we collected as we read in the last session. But today we will use those facts to infer.

Teach/Model

- We want kids to see that when we infer, we are really **"building a case" for our inference.**

- The focus question continues to function like a magnet as kids **use gathered facts and their background knowledge to make inferences.**

. . . Let's look back at the text, the facts we gathered, and our focus question.

. . . Turn and talk about what you notice.

. . . Let's continue to think and read about this topic. I'm going to start at the beginning of the text. (Read to a fact you noted previously.) I see we listed this as a fact on our chart. Reading this part and considering what I know helps me infer . . .

. . . I'm going to add another column to our chart so we can record our inferences. Keep in mind that when we infer, we are combining text clues and our own background knowledge. We are also keeping our focus question in mind.

QUESTION	
Facts	Inferences

. . . Turn and talk about a fact you found that leads you to infer.

. . . As I read, I am keeping our focus question in mind. (Read on.) This part of the text suggests that we might infer. Here's what I noticed in the text that supports my inference.

. . . Does everyone see how this works?

Guide/Support Practice

TEACHING MOVES

- Have kids **take notes and code their Post-its** (*F* for *fact*, *I* for *inference*) as they reread or continue reading.

- Remind kids to **keep the focus question in mind** as they work.

- Tell students that you want them to **reread, not just skim and scan** the text.

TEACHING LANGUAGE

. . . Now it's your turn. Use your Post-its as you reread (and read on, if you didn't finish). If you record a new fact, code your Post-it with an *F* for *fact*. If you infer, code the Post-it with an *I* for *inference*.

. . . Remember to keep the question in mind!

. . . Don't just skim and scan. Reread carefully. Notice the facts you identified, and note any new ones. Also think about what you can infer, using the text clues (the facts) and your background knowledge. Record the new facts and your inferences, and remember to code your Post-its.

. . . I will be around to listen to your reading and inferring.

Wrap Up

TEACHING MOVES

- Have kids **share their inferences** and add to the chart. Be sure kids can articulate the evidence that supports their inference.

- Help kids use the facts and inferences on the group chart to **draw conclusions and answer the focus question.**

TEACHING LANGUAGE

. . . Take a minute to turn and talk about what you learned and what you inferred.

. . . Let's see what we can add to our chart.

. . . So we have gathered facts and inferences to answer our focus question. Let's put our ideas together. What's the answer? What evidence supports our conclusions?

. . . Great thinking! So what we have done here is inferred an answer to our question using text evidence. We've drawn a conclusion based on the facts and information we read.

ASSESS AND PLAN

Did kids make inferences that were supported by evidence presented in the text?

This is an excellent lesson to use with a content-area text for further practice. The idea of asking a focus question and gathering evidence for making inferences to answer the question will strengthen content-area study and offer kids an opportunity to see how they can use the same strategies in reading, science, social studies, and other subjects.

Companion to . . .

The Comprehension Toolkit
Lesson 12: Tackle the Meaning
of Language

Session Goals

We want students to:
- use the context and background knowledge to infer meaning from the poem's words, lines, and phrases.
- gain an understanding of how to move beyond a literal interpretation using the strategy of inferring.
- articulate their understanding by sharing their inferences, questions, and interpretations of the poem's deeper meaning.

Infer the Meaning of Poems

In *The Comprehension Toolkit* Lesson 12, students learn to infer beyond the literal meaning of nonfiction poems. The companion session for Lesson 12 offers kids more time and support to practice inferring with nonfiction poems.

Text Matters

Poems make great texts for this session. Poetry is by its very nature an economy of words. Robert Frost said that poetry "begins in delight and ends in wisdom."

We want to choose poems that have lots of gaps or "holes" for kids to fill in with inferences and visual images. Many poems by Langston Hughes, Pat Mora, and David McCord leave readers something to think about. "The World Is an Open Book" from *Toolkit Texts: Grades 2–3* and poems from *Honey, I Love* by Eloise Greenfield also invite readers to infer meaning.

Select two poems so students can read one together and one independently.

Considerations for Planning

Poetry demands a full response from the reader. It has been said that poems demand we meet them halfway. By offering kids poems, we offer them authentic reasons to bring their own interpretations to a text and infer the meaning that is tucked inside the economical but rich language of poetry. Students learn that by slowing down their reading, they can dig deeply into words, phrases, and images.

Write the first poem on a chart so everyone can see it.

Students will need individual copies of the second poem.

Build Background, Word and Concept Knowledge

■ We want kids to see that **poems can be about many topics** and ideas, including nonfiction.

■ We **invite kids to read and respond to a poem.**

. . . Today we will look at a wonderful poem. Perhaps you haven't thought of poetry as nonfiction, but often poets draw their ideas from the world around them.

. . . A poet uses fewer words than an author of prose, the writing we are most familiar with in our everyday reading and writing.

. . . Because poetry has fewer words and is sometimes ambiguous or unclear in meaning, we readers have to work a bit harder and infer to interpret the meaning of a poem.

. . . When we infer the meaning of the poet's words, we may uncover the deeper meaning that the poet is trying to express. Then we really understand poetry!

Teach/Model

- Reading poetry is such an invitation for kids to dig into the words! **Poems are perfect for inferring and** creating mind pictures, or **visualizing.**

- Give students an opportunity to slow their reading down and **consider the deeper meaning** contained in a few words.

. . . Let's look at the poem I've selected. I have it written on a chart so we can all see the words.

. . . Let's read the poem all the way through—we'll do a choral reading of it! Poetry needs to be read out loud!

. . . I want to show you how we can read a poem, and, as we do, we can code the text or write our inferences right beside the words or phrases of the poem. We can also sketch a picture of the visual image the words create in our mind. (Model this.)

. . . Let me begin reading, and, as I do, I will stop and share my thinking. Because poems have few words, we have lots of opportunities to infer, using our own background knowledge and experiences along with the text clues. (Begin reading and coding the text. You can remind kids about the inferring equation, TC + BK = I, as you infer and visualize.)

. . . Turn and talk about something you noticed and inferred, or a visual image the words created in your mind.

. . . As I read, I am keeping my background knowledge in mind. I'm also thinking about questions that the poem raises in my mind. (Complete the poem.)

. . . Turn and talk about what you noticed.

Guide/Support Practice

TEACHING MOVES

- **Give students another poem.** Read it together.

- Invite kids to **share their initial thinking** before they code their own poems.

- Be sure students understand how to **slow their reading down, stop to infer, and code the text.**

TEACHING LANGUAGE

. . . I have another poem for you to read. Let's read through it together first. Poems are really best read aloud when we first read them. (Read a second poem that each student has a copy of.)

. . . Turn and talk about your initial thinking about the poem, especially your inferences or visual images.

. . . Share some of your ideas. Great!

. . . Now I want you to reread the poem, thinking about what you are inferring, and code the text and sketch any visual images to show your thinking.

. . . I will be around to listen and to help if you need me.

Wrap Up

TEACHING MOVES

- **Have students share their coding** and the inferences they made.

- As they share, **record their thinking and the strategies they used** to infer.

TEACHING LANGUAGE

. . . Take a minute to turn and talk about what you inferred.

. . . Let's code (draw or write) our shared thinking right on a copy of the poem.

. . . Great thinking today! You learned that by slowing down your reading, you could see meaning in the poem that wasn't so obvious when you first read it. You inferred as you read to unlock the meaning of the words and phrases, and you created visual images, too. Using both these strategies helped us understand the poem so much better!

ASSESS AND PLAN

Did kids understand that by reading the poem slowly, they saw deeper meaning in the poem?

Often kids have had little experience with poetry. Reading poems during read-aloud and shared reading and having baskets of poetry books in the room can ease access to uncovering the deeper meaning in poetry.

As students read, check to make sure they:

- monitor their understanding and leave tracks of their thinking as they "code the poem."
- stop, think, react, and ask questions as they read poetry.
- merge their background knowledge with text clues to make inferences and visualize to uncover the poem's meaning.

Infer the Meaning of Subheads

> *The basic goals of reading are to enable children to gain an understanding of the world and of themselves.* (Tierney, Readence, and Dishner, 1995)

Companion to . . .

The Comprehension Toolkit
Lesson 13: Crack Open Features

In *The Comprehension Toolkit* Lesson 13, students learn to infer the meaning of inferential subheads and titles. The companion session for Lesson 13 offers students a review of standard and inferential subheads and the opportunity to practice inferring with subheads as they read selected articles.

TEXT MATTERS

We select articles that have subheads for each section so kids see that they can use both the title and subheads to prepare to read a text. Consider selecting two short articles: one with standard (explicit) subheads and one with inferential subheads so kids have an opportunity to read both.

"Buried Alive!" and "The Comeback Humpbacks" in the *Source Book of Short Text*, "Jai Alai" and "Living at the Bottom of the World" in *Toolkit Texts: Grades 4–5*, and "The Horse Up Close" and "Rock Secrets" in *Toolkit Texts: Grades 2–3* are organized with subheads.

CONSIDERATIONS FOR PLANNING

Standard subheads are direct and explicit and reveal the text structure. For example, subheads that ask questions indicate a question-answer structure. The reader knows that what follows a boldface question will be the answer to that question. Other subheads and titles are less revealing and call on readers to infer what will follow, using their background knowledge and experience.

Kids need to learn how to use both types of subheads. We show them how to recognize the difference and make inferences when titles and subheads are less explicit and straightforward.

Students will need Post-its for this session.

SESSION GOALS

We want students to:

- understand the purpose of subheads and titles.
- use their background knowledge to infer the meaning of inferential subheads and titles.
- distinguish between standard and inferential subheads and titles.

Build Background, Word and Concept Knowledge

- **A careful explanation of the feature, *subheads*, is important.** Collect some texts that make use of various types of subheads. Show kids how some subheads are explicit, or straightforward, telling about the content that follows. We call these standard subheads. Other subheads may involve plays on words or catchy phrases that require the reader to infer what might follow. We call these inferential subheads.

- Be sure students understand the difference between *standard* subheads and *inferential* subheads.

. . . I have something so important to share with you. We have been looking at lots of nonfiction and finding ways to become more strategic as readers.

. . . You remember we talked about text and visual features earlier. (Consider having kids name a few: maps, charts, illustrations, etc.) Today we are going to explore a very useful feature: the *subhead*.

. . . I have gathered some examples of subheads. (Show some examples.) Some subheads tell the reader exactly what is coming in the text that follows. We call those *standard* subheads. Other subheads are not quite as straightforward, so the reader has to infer what the author plans to convey in that section. We call those *inferential* subheads. Both kinds, however, guide the reader by capturing an idea to briefly indicate what will follow in the text.

. . . So there are really two kinds of subheads: subheads that are clear and specific like this one (show an example) and others like this one (show an example) that are a little vague, or involve a play on words or a clever phrase.

Teach/Model

- **Introduce the text** and point out the subheads. Preview any pertinent vocabulary.

- **Sometimes readers read right over subheads.** They haven't yet realized that a subhead holds information that tells them in advance what a section of the text will be about.

- **Make sure to model both types of subheads,** even if you must use two short articles. You can have kids read one during the small-group session, and the other as independent practice followed by discussion at the beginning of the next small-group session.

. . . Let's look at the text I have selected. You notice that it has subheads because the author has used bold print to make sure we notice them.

. . . Before we read, let's talk about some vocabulary you'll need to know.

. . . Now I want to show you how we read, using the subheads to help us. (Begin previewing the text, using subheads to guide you.)

. . . I notice this subhead that says . . . I suspect that section will be about . . .

. . . Here's another . . .

. . . Turn and talk about what you think the author will include in this section.

. . . I notice that some of the subheads we are looking at are clearer than others in telling us what a section of the article will be about. For example, this one says . . . So, I am inferring that since the main title is . . . , this section might be about . . . . I'll jot my idea on a Post-it and mark the subhead with an *I* because I have to *infer.*

. . . As I read, I am keeping background knowledge in mind *and* thinking about whether the author has used a standard or inferential subhead.

. . . Turn and talk about what you are noticing.

Guide/Support Practice

- **Have students read,** using Post-its to record and code their thinking.

- Be sure kids feel confident in their task. If some students seem confused, **offer support.**

. . . I want you to continue reading in this article. As you read, put a Post-it beside each subhead and jot a very brief description of what you think the section is about. Code each subhead with an *S* for *standard* or an *I* for *inferential.*

. . . I will be around to help you if you need me.

Wrap Up

- **Have students share their coding.**

- **Help them explain** what they are learning about subheads.

. . . Take a minute to turn and talk about what you found.

. . . Great thinking today! You learned that subheads are very helpful to us as readers. We use them to determine what that section of the text will be about. Often a subhead gives us the big idea of what a section is about. Then the details follow in the paragraphs in that section.

. . . (Optional) I'm going to give you this other short article we looked at to read on your own. Do the same thing with your Post-its, and we'll discuss what you did next time we meet.

ASSESS AND PLAN

Did students understand the difference between the two types of subheads?

If kids need more support understanding the two types of subheads, consider creating a sort. Sorts are terrific ways to help kids group things in bigger categories. Cut out ten or so examples of subheads with the text that follows, including both types—standard and inferential—and have kids sort by standard and inferential subheads. This will help kids clarify the difference. We want them to be clear about each type so they can be strategic as they read the information that follows.

Infer Answers to Authentic Questions

In *The Comprehension Toolkit* Lesson 14, students ask authentic questions during an interactive read-aloud. They read to find answers by inferring and discuss the strategies they used to answer their questions. The companion session for Lesson 14 offers kids more time and support to practice asking authentic questions and inferring answers as they read another text.

Companion to . . .

The Comprehension Toolkit
Lesson 14: Read with a Question
in Mind

TEXT MATTERS

For this session we select a text that encourages kids to ask authentic questions and read to find answers.

Short nonfiction articles work well, such as "Our Exciting Solar Neighborhood" or "Making Art Out of Junk: Meet the Artist" in *Toolkit Texts: Grades 2–3*. These offer intriguing information on topics about which kids are likely to have some background knowledge that will help them ask questions and infer answers.

Kids also need to read books that address important ideas and issues. For independent or guided reading that takes place over several days, consider engaging books like *Living Color* by Steve Jenkins or challenging books like *Starry Messenger: Galileo Galilei* by Peter Sís. These evoke thoughtful, authentic questions that compel kids to combine their background knowledge with the author's powerful ideas.

CONSIDERATIONS FOR PLANNING

Students often encounter questions at the end of their reading designed to "test" their reading comprehension. When we ask such questions, we are looking at the "end product" of reading. But we know that reading is so much more than just answering questions at the end. Questions that are authentic and kept in mind during reading propel the reader forward, creating a purpose for reading.

Students will need Post-its for this session.

SESSION GOALS

We want students to:

- ask authentic questions.
- read to find answers to their questions through inferring.
- discuss the strategies used to answer their questions.

Build Background, Word and Concept Knowledge

- We want kids to see that **as they engage with compelling ideas in interesting texts, questions arise naturally.** We show kids how their own background knowledge, combined with the new information they are learning, prompts authentic questions.

. . . Today we will see how we read to answer the authentic, natural questions that come to mind as we read.

. . . Sometimes our questions aren't answered directly in the text, and we have to infer answers to those questions.

Teach/Model

- **Introduce the text, engaging kids with the topic.** Have kids activate their background knowledge and discuss what they know about the topic.

- **Preview any pertinent vocabulary.**

- **List initial questions** as kids identify what they are wondering.

> ## Questions about . . .

- **Model how you keep the questions in mind as you read.** Make notes on Post-its as you find or infer answers.

. . . I have a very interesting text for us today!

. . . You know, when we begin reading about a topic, we get interested and some of our own questions surface that make us want to read on.

. . . Let's take a look at the text. Turn and talk about what you know about this topic.

. . . Here's some vocabulary we need to know.

. . . As I begin to read the text, I am already wondering . . . . I'm going to write my question on an anchor chart.

. . . As I look at this photo (illustration), I have another question . . . .

. . . What are you wondering about? Turn and talk.

. . . I hear you talking about questions you have, too. Let's record those on our chart.

. . . Notice how I keep these questions in mind as I read. (Read the text.) Right here, I'm thinking about the information and inferring an answer to the question . . . . I'll write my answer on a Post-it. Then I can put it next to the question on the chart.

. . . And look, here I found more information to help me answer a question. (Do another, or continue the same, example.)

. . . Remember, I am inferring. I used clues from the text and combined these with my background knowledge to figure out an answer to my question. Sometimes I infer using the photos or illustrations in the text as well as the words.

Guide/Support Practice

- **Have kids read,** recording their questions and answers on Post-its.

- **Offer support as needed.** Be sure kids understand that asking authentic questions not only encourages them to keep reading to look for answers, but also helps them combine the information they find with their own background knowledge to infer answers.

. . . Continue reading now, and we will talk about what you've found after you've read.

. . . I will be around to help you if you need me.

Wrap Up

- **Have students share their questions and the strategies they used** to find answers.

- **Make an anchor chart** to record the strategies kids used. Prompt kids to consider how they used visual and text features as well as words (text clues) to answer their questions.

- Also **discuss how they used their background knowledge and text clues,** as well as talking to each other, to figure out answers. (Review strategies kids learned in previous sessions.)

. . . Let's create another anchor chart to list all the strategies we used to answer questions.

When we read
to answer our questions . . .

ASSESS AND PLAN

Do students understand that often the answers to their questions aren't explicit in the text and they must use their background knowledge and experiences plus the text clues to determine an answer?

Because the questions we ask as we read are authentic questions, bubbling up from our reading, they often are less clear-cut than the questions kids are used to being asked. Offer kids Post-its to use in their independent reading to record their questions and answers. Use those in conferring with individual students to increase kids' tolerance of ambiguity and the need to either infer an answer or do further research.

Were students able to explain the strategies they used to answer their questions?

To assess how well kids understand that their inferences support them as readers to answer their questions, we post a few of their questions and answers on a chart, and they elaborate on how they inferred using text clues to answer their questions. We only ask kids to elaborate on a few examples and their process of inferring as the point is to articulate and explain their thinking, not "fill out" the chart.

Question	Answer	How I inferred to answer this question

Theme is the idea that holds the story together, such as a comment about either society, human nature, or the human condition.
(Lehr, 1991)

Companion to . . .

The Comprehension Toolkit
Lesson 15: Wrap Your Mind Around
the Big Ideas

Infer Themes from Text Evidence

In *The Comprehension Toolkit* Lesson 15, students learn the difference between plot and theme by considering the familiar story of "The Three Little Pigs." Then, during an interactive read-aloud of an historical-fiction story, they use text evidence to infer themes and support their interpretations. The two companion sessions for Lesson 15 help kids break down this process. In this first session, students focus on understanding the difference between plot and theme in another familiar story.

TEXT MATTERS

In this session, students will consider a familiar story such as "Goldilocks and the Three Bears," for which they will not need a text.

For the following session, you will select a sophisticated historical-fiction story that offers kids rich ideas and themes. Suggestions are offered in Session 15b.

SESSION GOAL

We want students to:

■ understand the difference between plot and theme.

CONSIDERATIONS FOR PLANNING

Students often confuse plot and theme. The plot of a story is what happens—events as they unfold. The characters' motives and actions connect to events and move the story forward. As proficient readers move through stories, they connect events and characters' behaviors to a central idea—a theme.

Themes are rarely explicit; most are inferred. When students infer themes in a text, we want them to gather evidence from the words, characters' actions, events, and ideas to support these themes.

This session revisits the distinction between plot and theme introduced in *The Comprehension Toolkit* Lesson 15.

Build Background, Word and Concept Knowledge

- We want to be sure kids have a clear understanding of **the difference between *plot* and *theme*.** In the next session, we will build on that understanding.

. . . All of you have read stories. When you do, you follow the story's events and the characters' actions. Those events and actions are part of the *plot* of the story.

. . . You also read stories to glean important ideas, messages the author wants readers to understand. Those big ideas are the *themes* of the story.

Teach/Model

- **Create an anchor chart** to record ideas about plot and theme. Helping kids understand and distinguish between the unfolding action and events of a story (the plot) and the important, enduring ideas (the themes) is important and will serve kids well as they mature as readers.

- **Explain that themes are often abstract.** In a fable the ending may state the moral or lesson, but in most stories the reader must infer the themes from the parts of the story.

- **Use a familiar story to illustrate** the difference between plot and theme. We use "Goldilocks and the Three Bears."

. . . So, let's learn these two important terms: *plot* and *theme*. We'll create an anchor chart to show the difference.

. . . When you read a story, you keep track of what is happening—how the story events unfold. We call that the *plot*. I will write the term *plot* in the first column of our chart and record what a plot is.

. . . *Theme* is different. A theme is a big idea, an idea you are left thinking about when the story ends. Many stories have more than one theme. Let's add *themes* to our chart.

Plot and Theme—What's the difference?

Plot =
what happens

Theme =
important ideas
(messages, lessons)

. . . Rarely do authors say explicitly, "This story is about friendship and the cycle of life." Authors leave the work of inferring themes up to us.

. . . Let's investigate plot and themes in a story you all know: "Goldilocks and the Three Bears." (This one works well, but other familiar stories will also work.)

. . . Let's tell that story. (Have kids help you retell the story and link the characters' behavior, the events, and the cultural and historical setting to the themes as you go. Wait for the discussion in Guide/Support Practice to record on the chart.)

. . . So, what are the themes in this story?

Guide/Support Practice

TEACHING MOVES	TEACHING LANGUAGE
■ **This session helps kids understand the terms *plot* and *theme*** in preparation for the more sophisticated story we will read in the next session.	. . . Turn and talk about what you noticed about the plot and themes of the story.
	. . . Let's record your ideas on our anchor chart.
■ **Help kids see that there are often multiple themes** that can be inferred in a story.	. . . In our next meeting, we will read a thoughtful story that I know you will enjoy. We'll be using our understanding of theme and plot as we read.

Wrap Up

TEACHING MOVES	TEACHING LANGUAGE
■ **Have students summarize** the discussion of theme and plot.	. . . Today we learned two important new terms about the way a story is structured. Turn and talk about what you learned.
	. . . Who can summarize what we learned?
	. . . We'll need these concepts in our next meeting. Keep them in mind as you read in your independent books, too!
	. . . Good thinking today!

ASSESS AND PLAN

Are students clear about the difference between plot and theme?
If you think there might be confusion, support students in considering plot and themes in another quick, familiar story before beginning the book in the next session.

> *Instead of functioning as a rigid mold, the text is seen to serve as a pattern, which the reader must to some extent create even as he is guided by it.* (Rosenblatt, 1978)

Companion to . . .

The Comprehension Toolkit
Lesson 15: Wrap Your Mind Around
the Big Ideas

Support Themes with Text Evidence

This session builds on the previous one. Students infer themes in a sophisticated story and support their themes with evidence from the text.

TEXT MATTERS

For this session we want to choose a text that will engage students in thinking about important ideas that evoke responses. We want kids to grapple with important issues, so we select a text that centers on ideas and issues.

Historical fiction and realistic fiction picture books work well. Select a book with brief text yet sophisticated themes, such as *Barefoot: Escape on the Underground Railroad* by Pamela Duncan Edwards. Or select a longer story and focus on a part that contains evidence of themes, such as the beginning of *Smoky Night* by Eve Bunting. Books with strong story elements and illustrations propel kids to read on and gather evidence from the text and pictures to support or revise inferences about themes.

Kids also need to read longer stories and books that make them think about big ideas. For independent reading, consider provocative, engaging books like *The Wednesday Surprise* by Eve Bunting or, for a challenging text, *Encounter* by Jane Yolen. These are rich in plot and character elements that help kids infer the themes.

CONSIDERATIONS FOR PLANNING

In this session, we help kids use their understanding of theme and plot in a complex story. We teach kids to think about the characters' words and actions as clues, or evidence, that support them to infer themes.

Have on hand the *Plot and Theme—What's the difference* anchor chart from the previous session.

Students will need individual copies of the *Evidence/My Thinking/Themes* chart used in this session.

SESSION GOALS

We want students to:

- recognize that we look at words, actions, events, ideas, and pictures in the text to infer themes.
- support their themes with evidence from the text.

Build Background, Word and Concept Knowledge

- We **check kids' understanding of theme and plot,** recalling the simple story used in the previous session to illustrate the difference.

. . . Last time we met, we talked about two ideas about stories: *plot* and *theme*.

. . . Turn and talk about what you recall. (Use the anchor chart from the previous session to review.)

> ### Plot and Theme—What's the difference?
>
> | Plot = | Theme = |
> |---|---|
> | what happens | important ideas (messages, lessons) |

. . . Today we'll have an opportunity to apply our learning in a new story.

Teach/Model

- **Introduce the book.** If the story involves a cultural or historical event, help kids gain access by telling them something about the period or event. For example, *Smoky Night* by Eve Bunting is the story of the Los Angeles riots. Kids need to know something about the cultural and racial differences that were at the heart of the event.

- **Begin to read and think aloud.** Model how readers pay close attention to plot developments, words, illustrations, characters and their actions, and the cultural and historical setting of the story to infer the developing themes.

- Model how to use the *Evidence/My Thinking/ Themes* group chart to **record text evidence and your thinking** as you read.

- Tell kids they need to **read on for a bit before they can begin inferring themes.**

. . . Let me tell you a little about this story. (Provide students with enough information to get started. You may want to read something about the book from the flap or back of the book.)

. . . As I read, I am going to share how I link the themes I am inferring to evidence in the text. We'll make a chart to record.

Evidence	My Thinking	Themes
(words, actions, ideas, illustrations from the text)	(inferences, questions, connections)	

. . . Let's read a few pages together before you read on your own. (Read some of the story.)

. . . I'm going to begin by recording (the words, characters' actions) I read right here . . . . This is evidence from the text. I'll record it in the first column.

. . . Now I'll share my thinking; I'll jot it in the middle column: I infer . . .

. . . Turn and talk about what you are noticing. (Jot down observations about the story and kids' inferences or questions.)

. . . We have to get into the story a little more before we begin inferring themes.

Guide/Support Practice

- **Give kids individual copies** of the *Evidence/ My Thinking/Themes* chart.

- Review the task to check for understanding. **Work with students** until they see themes emerging.

- **Have kids continue on their own.** Move among them in case some need additional support.

. . . We will continue reading together. I'm going to give each of you a chart to record evidence from the text and our thinking. Let's try a bit together, and then you'll be on your own. (Continue reading and recording with kids until some themes begin to emerge.)

. . . Let's stop here and review our evidence and our thinking. What are some themes that are beginning to emerge?

. . . So do you see that as we thought about the words, ideas, and characters' actions, we began to surface the themes in this story?

. . . Now you're ready to continue reading and recording on your own. I'll be around to listen and help.

Wrap Up

- **Have students share** their responses, and record them on the anchor chart.

. . . What a great story! Let's share the evidence we found in the story that supports the themes we came up with. Turn and talk with each other first.

. . . Maybe someone thought of a theme that is really central to the story. Any suggestions? We can think of the theme first and then go back and find evidence that supports it. (Add themes and evidence to the group chart.)

. . . You did a good job of surfacing the themes that were emerging as you read and linking them to text evidence.

. . . This will be really helpful in your own independent reading, too!

Assess and Plan

Are students able to apply their understanding of plot and theme with a sophisticated story?

The process of inferring themes is a sophisticated one that kids need a lot of practice to master. Use read-aloud and independent reading conferences to help kids grow more confident.

Infer Meaning

After this unit, you want to know that students make inferences and create visual images to better understand what they are reading, so your conference should help the student talk about how she or he infers and visualizes during reading—answering questions, surfacing big ideas, and gaining deeper meaning.

1. **Invite the student to choose a passage and create a context for it.**
   - Choose a part of your book to read to me.
   - *(If the student doesn't stop to make inferences or describe visual images on his or her own)* What inferences and/or mental images did you make as you read?

2. **Focus on the inferences and visual images the student created as she or he read.**
   - Share some of the inferences you made as you read. Tell me about the visual images you created in your mind as you read.
   - Show me something you wrote down or sketched that you inferred or visualized as you read the words, phrases, or sentences in the text. Tell me about it.
   - Show me a part of the text that was difficult to understand, and tell me how you inferred or visualized to better understand it. Tell me about how you combined clues in the text with your background knowledge to make an inference.
   - *(If reading a nonfiction text with features, including subheads and titles)* Tell me about a place where you inferred to learn from a visual or text feature.

3. **Ask the student to continue reading, sharing any questions that may have come up.**
   - Show me a place where you found yourself asking a question.
   - Tell me about how you made an inference to answer your question.

Conference Recording Form for "Infer Meaning," located in "Resources" section.

4. **Ask the student to think about the overall meaning of the text.**
   - Share what you inferred are the big ideas or themes in this piece.
   - Tell me about or show me some evidence in the text that supports the big idea(s) or the theme(s) you came up with.

Reading Conference Recording Form: Infer Meaning

Name _____ Date _____

Book title _____

GOAL	EVIDENCE
The student . . .	This student . . .
1. Understands the text • Tells what the book is about and talks about what he or she was thinking while reading	
2. Is aware of his or her own visualizing and inferring strategies • Describes and explains inferences and mental images • Combines text clues with background knowledge to understand a difficult part • (If reading nonfiction with features) Infers information from features	
3. Infers to answer questions • Asks a question and makes inferences to answer it	
4. Infers and visualizes to surface big ideas and themes • Uses inferring and visualizing to surface big ideas and themes • Supports big ideas and themes with text evidence	

Follow-Ups

If a student has difficulty with any of the primary goals in this unit, prompts like the following may be helpful during independent work in subsequent units.

- What are you thinking? What are you inferring or visualizing?
- How did you make meaning as you read these words/phrases/sentences?
- How might inferring help you figure out that part of the text?
- Are you creating pictures in your mind that help you understand the text?
- Any questions? Did you infer or visualize to answer that question?
- What are the big ideas and/or themes here?
- What evidence from the text supports that theme or big idea?

Language students may use to demonstrate that they are inferring meaning

- I infer . . . I think . . . Maybe . . .
- I am creating a picture in my mind right here.
- I combined my background knowledge with text clues to make an inference, so I infer that . . .
- These words paint a picture in my mind. They make me feel, see, hear . . .
- I think this part means . . .
- This part answered my question. I inferred that . . .
- This information makes me think . . .
- The theme here is . . . The big idea is . . . based on these words in the text: . . .
- The evidence in the text that supports the big idea/theme is . . .

Determine Importance

What we determine to be important in a text depends on our purpose for reading it. When we read nonfiction, we are reading to learn and remember information. We can't possibly remember every isolated fact, nor should we. We need to focus on important information and merge it with what we already know to expand our understanding of a topic. We sort and sift rich details from important information to answer questions and arrive at main ideas. We identify details that support larger concepts. We teach kids a way to use information to develop a line of thinking as they read, surfacing and focusing their attention on important ideas in the text.

> *Determining importance*
> *has to do with knowing why*
> *you're reading and then*
> *making decisions about which*
> *information or ideas are most*
> *critical to understanding the*
> *overall meaning of the piece.*
> (Zimmermann and
> Hutchins, 2003)

Record Facts, Questions, and Responses

In *The Comprehension Toolkit* Lesson 16, students use a *Facts/Questions/ Responses (FQR)* chart to take notes and merge their thinking with new information as they respond to a read-aloud article. The two companion sessions for Lesson 16 give kids more support and practice with this process. In this first session, students work with the teacher to use an *FQR* chart as they read another article together.

Companion to . . .

The Comprehension Toolkit
Lesson 16: Spotlight New Thinking

TEXT MATTERS

To launch *FQR* charts, we select a text that engages kids with their background knowledge, but takes them beyond to learn new information. The new information invites them to respond in a variety of ways.

A short, accessible text that has interesting facts to record works well. Selections such as "The Passion of Cesar Chavez" in the *Source Book of Short Text*, "Moon Walking" and "You Can Do Yoga" in *Toolkit Texts: Grades 2–3*, and "How Do We Taste?" in *Toolkit Texts: Grades 6–7* provide enough facts to stimulate kids' questions.

CONSIDERATIONS FOR PLANNING

The *Facts/Questions/Responses (FQR)* chart offers a thoughtful, useful alternative to traditional note taking. In the past, students have been taught to take notes by simply recording the facts. The *FQR* chart encourages kids to actually consider the impact of the new information on their background knowledge. Instead of just jotting facts, they stop and think about the information—connecting to it, wondering about it, and reacting to it. The *FQR* chart can accompany students into all their content area classrooms to help them learn and remember as they take notes.

Prepare a few note cards with isolated facts to show kids that approach so they can contrast it with the *FQR* form.

SESSION GOALS

We want students to:

- understand that merely jotting down the facts isn't enough, and that recording their questions and responses helps them better understand what they read.
- include a variety of responses such as connections, reactions, and inferences.

Build Background, Word and Concept Knowledge

- **Invite kids to skim and scan** to get a sense of the article. Skimming and scanning for key ideas helps kids organize their background information in advance and merge it with new information as they read.

- **Preview new vocabulary** or concepts to make sure kids grasp the meaning of these before reading.

- **Show a few sample note cards** with isolated facts written on them to illustrate how students are often taught to take notes. This will help kids see the contrast and the utility of the *FQR* chart.

- **Introduce the *FQR* chart.**

. . . I have an interesting article for us to read today. I read it and was so fascinated by all the interesting ideas in it that I knew you would like it!

. . . Take a moment to skim and scan the article. Turn and talk when you finish. (Skim with kids if needed.)

. . . Here's a word you'll need to know . . . .

. . . When we read, figuring out information and keeping track of it is really important. I'm going to share something with you that I find extremely helpful for thinking about and remembering information.

. . . Let me show you how I used to take notes—and how I take them now! (Show note cards with isolated facts.) When I was in school, I took notes this way, but, honestly, I never found note cards very useful. Now I've found a way that is so much more helpful! It is called the *FQR* chart.

. . . Here's how the *FQR* chart works. (Show the chart.) It has three columns: *Facts*, *Questions*, and *Responses*. When I am reading, I use this form to take my notes. Unlike those cards you saw, this form really helps me connect to information so I can learn it! The *F* in *FQR* is for *facts* that we find as we read. The *Q* is for *questions* we have about words and ideas, and the *R* column is where we record our *responses* and *reactions*—our inferences, what we are thinking, and how we might be feeling. I'll show you how to use this form as we read today.

Teach/Model

- Show kids how you **record using the** *FQR* **chart.**

- **It is important to think aloud** for kids because this is a new way of thinking about note taking.

- In recording facts, show kids how you **capture the essence of the idea** with as few words as possible.

- **Demonstrate that responses can be wide-ranging** and include everything from noticing the way the author presents the information to how you think you'll make use of it.

- **Show how questions arise** as we learn new facts, and also from our responses.

. . . I'm going to think aloud as I read so you can see how I use the *FQR* chart.

Facts	Questions	Responses

. . . Listen as I read the first part. Now that I have read a paragraph (or a section, but not too much), I will stop and record some facts. I have to select the facts I want to write down. I can't write everything, so I write the facts that I want to remember, using as few words as possible to capture the idea. (Model how you think about the facts, being selective.)

. . . Now that I've written these facts, I have a response to this information. I listen for my inner conversation to prompt me when I am reading, and I record that in the *Responses* column.

. . . Or sometimes when I learn some new information, I have a question. (Model.)

. . . Turn and talk about what you are thinking.

. . . Let's read on. (Continue modeling how to use the *FQR* chart.)

. . . Turn and talk about how the *FQR* chart works.

Guide/Support Practice

- **Have kids read along with you,** but continue to guide them and record their ideas on the group chart. This extra support and guidance will help them will feel much more confident in the next session, when you offer them the opportunity to use their own chart.

. . . You try it now, and I will record your facts, questions, and responses. Read the next two paragraphs.

. . . Let's record your thoughts on our chart.

. . . Let's read on to the end now.

. . . As we read, we will add to our *Facts/Questions/ Responses* chart.

Wrap Up

- **Have students discuss** the process of using the *FQR* chart. Be sure they understand how the three columns capture different aspects of their reading and thinking.

- **Make sure kids understand** how facts, questions, and responses are connected across the columns. This in turn helps them understand and remember the information.

. . . Share your thinking about using the *FQR* chart.

. . . Good thinking! You are seeing how when we read and record facts, that reading and those facts often lead to responses and even to questions.

. . . Next time we meet, we'll read another article, and you will create your own *FQR* chart.

ASSESS AND PLAN

What did you notice from students' sharing? Are there aspects of the process about which they seem less confident?

Use students' sharing as a quick assessment to determine what you might need to review in the following session before they use the *FQR* chart on their own. Plan to include a review of any part of the process about which students seem insecure. In the next session, we want them to be confident in their use of the *FQR* chart.

Make sure students can:

- distinguish between facts, questions, and responses.
- explain how each is important to understanding the text.

> *Children with strong belief in their own agency work harder, focus their attention better, are more interested in their studies, and are less likely to give up when they encounter difficulties.*
> (Johnston, 2004)

Companion to . . .

The Comprehension Toolkit
Lesson 16: Spotlight New Thinking

Take Notes on an *FQR* Chart

This session builds on the previous one. Students use the *FQR* chart independently with a new text.

TEXT MATTERS

When we have students use their own *FQR* charts, we want to select an engaging text, but one that is accessible. Freeing kids' thinking energy from decoding challenges gives them more energy for understanding and using the *FQR* process in their initial attempt.

Select another short, interesting article for kids to read. Selections such as "Ancient Mexico" and "The Struggle for Equal Rights" in *Toolkit Texts: Grades 4–5*, "Flying Again" in *Toolkit Texts: Grades 2–3*, and "The Case Against Soda" in the *Source Book of Short Text* provide enough facts to stimulate kids' questions and responses.

SESSION GOALS

We want students to:
- merge their thinking on an *FQR* chart to take notes when reading nonfiction.
- include a variety of responses such as connections, reactions, and inferences.

CONSIDERATIONS FOR PLANNING

We introduced the *Facts/Questions/Responses (FQR)* chart in the previous session with a solid demonstration of how it works. In this session, we invite kids to use their own *FQR* chart with a short text. After a brief introduction of the text and a model of one paragraph, we have kids work independently with guided support as needed.

Have on hand the group *FQR* chart from the previous session.

Students will need individual *FQR* charts for this session.

Build Background, Word and Concept Knowledge

TEACHING MOVES

- **Provide any review** you think is necessary, based on kids' discussion and your observations from the previous session. Show the *FQR* chart from the previous session.

- **Invite kids to skim the new article** as they did in the previous session. This is a great strategy to help kids develop. Previewing is so productive, some say that nonfiction reading requires we spend almost as much time "planning to read" as we do reading!

- **Preview pertinent vocabulary** or concepts kids need to know before they read.

TEACHING LANGUAGE

. . . I have another interesting article for us to read today. Remember when we last met and read, we used the *FQR* chart to capture our thinking.

. . . Who can remind us how the *FQR* chart works? (Show the chart made in the previous session.)

. . . Now take a few moments to skim the new article. Turn and talk when you finish.

. . . What did you notice about the article? What do you know about the topic that would be helpful for you to consider as you begin to read?

. . . Let's talk about some words you need to know before you read.

Teach/Model

TEACHING MOVES

- **Keep the FQR chart** from the previous session in view for reference.

- **Give kids small versions** of the *FQR* chart. A form is located on page 69 of *The Comprehension Toolkit* Strategy Book 5: *Determine Importance*, or kids can make their own charts by folding a blank sheet of paper in thirds and writing headers for each column.

- In providing the model, **use a small chart yourself.** This will keep kids from feeling they should copy what you write.

TEACHING LANGUAGE

. . . Today you will make your own *FQR* chart as you read. Think about how we jotted information in the three columns. Who can share what we did?

. . . We can start off together. I'll read the first paragraph of our new article and share my thinking. (Read aloud.)

. . . Now, I'll jot some things on my chart while you do the same.

. . . Turn and talk about what you are thinking and share what you wrote.

. . . Great! Let's get started reading on our own.

Guide/Support Practice

TEACHING MOVES

- **Have kids read and record** on their own. If some students seem unsure, offer side-by-side support.

TEACHING LANGUAGE

. . . Record your facts, questions, and responses.

. . . Be sure to pace yourself, stopping every paragraph or two to think about what you are reading and to record on the chart.

. . . Read on now, and I will be around to listen in and help if you need me.

Wrap Up

- **Have kids discuss** what they recorded on their personal *FQR* chart. Note similarities and differences in the charts. The "responses" column will often reflect more unique thoughts.

- **Encourage kids to recognize connections** among the columns on their charts. Have them draw arrows to show the connections in their thinking.

. . . Share your *FQR* charts with one another.

. . . I see information recorded in all three columns. Let's look a little more closely at what you wrote.

. . . Notice that you are more likely to really think about the fact and remember it if you had a question about it or a response to it.

. . . Remember, you can connect your thinking across the columns and show the connections with arrows. For example, you might connect a question and some information you found that answered it. Or connect a response that you had to some amazing information that you recorded in the *Facts* column. Draw an arrow from one column to another to show your connections. (Model.) Now you try it.

. . . Who has a connection you would like to share?

Assess and Plan

What did students' personal *FQR* charts reflect about their understanding of the process and content?

Use the *FQR* charts to assess kids' understanding. If confusions are present, consider offering another guided practice for students who may need the extra support.

Code a Text to Hold Your Thinking

In *The Comprehension Toolkit* Lesson 18, students learn to code a text to hold their thinking and paraphrase to record information. The two companion sessions for Lesson 18 offer kids more support and practice with this process. In this session, they focus on coding a text to leave tracks of their thinking, and they begin to practice paraphrasing and identifying important information.

TEXT MATTERS

We want students to approach with confidence texts that have lots of details and facts. They need to fully understand the information before they can determine the important ideas. Coding offers kids a management strategy for sifting and sorting information.

Short, informative articles such as "Buried Alive!" in the *Source Book of Short Text*, "Frog Watching" in *Toolkit Texts: Grades 6–7*, and "By Land, Sea, and Air" and "Animal Helpers" in *Toolkit Texts: Grades 2–3* lend themselves to coding.

The text used in *The Comprehension Toolkit* Lesson 18 is a lengthy, information-packed expository text. If you select a textbook chapter or other lengthy text for this session, we suggest continuing with the same text through Session 19. *National Geographic* books and periodicals provide good choices. Their leveled texts contain numerous facts and give kids a chance to see how much more manageable a text becomes with coding.

CONSIDERATIONS FOR PLANNING

Many texts are filled with what seems to kids to be an unmanageable number of facts to navigate. History and science textbooks often have such dense text that they have been called "inconsiderate" texts. Teaching kids to access their prior knowledge and code information as they read gives them strategies to manage text and increase their understanding and learning.

Students will need to write on their copies of the text.

Companion to . . .

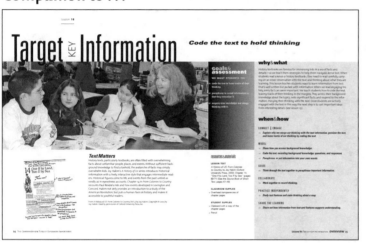

The Comprehension Toolkit
Lesson 18: Target Key Information

SESSION GOALS

We want students to:

- code the text to leave tracks of their thinking.
- include a variety of responses such as connections, reactions, and inferences.

Build Background, Word and Concept Knowledge

■ **Share the good news/bad news** about reading nonfiction. Nonfiction texts can be challenging for kids. Often, dense texts leave them trying to wade through myriad facts and details. Many readers try to sift and sort as they go, but they struggle with what to hold onto in their thinking as they make their way through a text. When we show students how to approach their reading in ways that make a text manageable, they find nonfiction engaging and packed with information they can conquer.

■ **This session incorporates many strategies** students have used previously. Referring back to previous sessions ("Remember when we . . .") helps kids become flexible readers and understand that well-learned strategies adapt to many reading experiences.

■ **Preview the text with kids,** including pertinent vocabulary or concepts central to the text's meaning.

■ **Introduce the word** *code* and the concept of coding a text.

. . . Today we will read a text that has lots of interesting information. "Lots of interesting information" is a good news/bad news story! I know you all love learning new information, and when you read something that has lots to learn in it, you are excited. That's the "good news!" The "bad news" is that sometimes we find lots of information hard to manage.

. . . I'm going to show you something we can do that will help us and make it *all* good news!

. . . Let's preview the text first. Take a few minutes to scan. Then turn and talk.

. . . There are some words you'll need to know in this text. Let's talk about this one.

. . . I hear you using your background knowledge already! That's perfect because you are remembering that accessing what we already know is the first step in reading nonfiction.

. . . How many of you have heard the word *code?* When we talk about codes, we usually are thinking about a system of words or letters that stands for something else.

. . . Today we will learn how we can code a text as we read to help us with the meaning. When we "code" something, we "transfer" or "translate" the message so we can better manage it.

. . . Our goal today is to code the text by leaving tracks of our own thinking in both words and symbols. We will write our thinking in the margins, right next to the words in the text.

Teach/Model

TEACHING MOVES

- **Make an anchor chart** to record and explain the codes. When we help kids identify the coding symbols, we give them a powerful tool to tackle dense texts. The chart will help in the next session as kids paraphrase information from the text using the notes and codes they have written in the margins.

- As you begin to read the text, model how you **use the codes and write notes** in the margins to keep track of your thinking.

- Point out that you **put information in your own words** as you write your notes.

- **Review the term** *paraphrase* and the concept of paraphrasing.

TEACHING LANGUAGE

. . . Let's make a chart to record and explain the codes we use.

Code	Why We Coded
BK	I have background knowledge.
*	I think this is important!
?	I have a question.
R	I have a response.
_____	I underline important info.

. . . Listen as I read the title . . . . I am going to put the abbreviation *BK* beside the title because I have some background knowledge about this. I'll add a few words to write down what I know right next to the title.

. . . As I read on, I notice that I have some background knowledge here, too, so I will write *BK* again and add some words to help me recall my connection.

. . . Turn and talk about what you are thinking.

. . . Hmmm . . . I have a question here. I will put a question mark, ?, and write my question.

. . . I'll read a little more. Wow! I think this is really important. I am going to code it with a star, *, so I will remember it. I'll *paraphrase* this information, or write it in my own words, in the margin.

. . . I also have a response, so I'll jot it and code with an *R*.

. . . Does everyone see how this works? Let's look back at the chart and the ways I used the codes as I read.

Guide/Support Practice

- **Have kids read on** in the text and code as they go.

- **If you notice confusion,** stop students and give additional guided support. If only one or two students experience difficulty, offer support to those students.

. . . You give it a try now. Record your thoughts as you read, using the codes we talked about. Make sure you put important information into your own words and write your thinking in the margins.

. . . Read on to the end. (If the text is lengthy, set an appropriate stopping place to check in or read to.)

. . . I will be around to help you.

Wrap Up

- **Have students discuss** the process of coding.

- **Have kids compare what they coded.** When kids compare, they will see that they have coded some similar things in terms of questions and importance. They will likely have differences, too. By having them compare, you can help them see that their thinking is important and that as readers differ, so do their responses. They'll also realize that slowing down their reading to stop, think, and respond makes the text much more manageable and understandable.

. . . Share your thinking about using coding and margin notes to manage texts with lots of information.

. . . Let's compare the ways in which you coded. What do you notice? Turn and talk.

. . . We're different as readers, so our coding may be different, and that's okay. Coding helps us to slow down and think about the text so we understand and learn more from our reading.

. . . Good work today! We will use the coding you did today in our next meeting, so stay tuned for more!

ASSESS AND PLAN

What did you notice about students' comfort and flexibility with coding?

Coding may seem awkward at first. Once students learn that there is not one "right" way to code the text, they learn to trust their own reactions and responses and develop confidence as readers. If, after this session, kids need more practice with coding and paraphrasing, continue with Session 18b. If they have a good grasp of how to code and paraphrase, you can move directly to Session 19, where students will use a note-taking scaffold to distinguish between important information and interesting details.

Companion to . . .

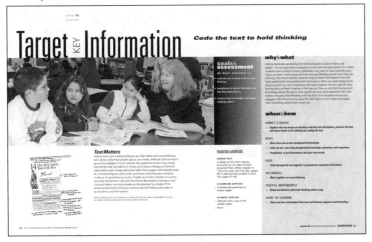

The Comprehension Toolkit
Lesson 18: Target Key Information

Paraphrase to Record Information

This session builds on the previous one. Students focus on paraphrasing the information they coded in the text to merge the new knowledge with their thinking and remember it.

TEXT MATTERS

In the previous session, we invited kids to code text. We modeled how to use symbols and brief annotations to note important facts and details, their own background knowledge to merge with the author's information, and questions they can pursue within and beyond the text.

In this session we continue with the same text, but we focus on teaching kids how to recognize important information and paraphrase ideas so they understand and learn.

CONSIDERATIONS FOR PLANNING

This session focuses on helping kids make use of their coding. So often, students jot down information in the author's words. We want kids to pay close attention to their inner conversation and code text in their own words as they locate new information, wonder, and connect their background knowledge.

We show students how to use their coding in paraphrasing so that the new information becomes their own.

Have on hand the anchor chart of codes used in the previous session.

Students will need their copies of the text they coded in the previous session.

Students will need Post-its.

SESSION GOALS

We want students to:

- paraphrase to record information so that they remember it.
- acquire new knowledge and merge thinking with it.
- begin to surface what's important as they read.

Build Background, Word and Concept Knowledge

- **Refresh students' thinking** about the coding they did in the previous session.

- Have them look back at the chart of codes and turn and **talk about how they used the codes.** Make sure they have the copy of the text they coded.

- **Review the term** *paraphrase* and the concept of paraphrasing.

. . . Today we will be rereading the text we coded when we last met. We will look at what we underlined in the text, what we wrote in the margins, and the coding we used.

. . . Here's the chart we made to show the different codes, or symbols we are using, and what they mean. Turn and talk about how you used these codes. Point out for each other where you used the codes in the text.

Code	Why We Coded
BK	I have background knowledge.
*	I think this is important!
?	I have a question.
R	I have a response.
_____	I underline important info.

. . . Today we're going to reread and *paraphrase* the information, or put it into our own words, to help us learn and remember it.

Teach/Model

■ Model how you **reread and paraphrase.** Show students how to look back over their coding to reconsider the importance of what they coded, to combine ideas with their own, and to paraphrase so they'll be more likely to remember.

■ **If you need more room** to paraphrase the information, use Post-its.

■ **Give kids questions** to keep in mind as they reread and paraphrase: "Can I combine ideas? Which ideas are really important? Are there questions I have? How does my background knowledge help here?"

. . . Let's look at my coding. Remember, I coded this part as *BK* because I already knew something that related. I also underlined some things. Now I will add what I know to what I underlined and coded as important and merge the two. Here's the way it sounds when I paraphrase it and make it my own words . . . . Watch as I write it here. (Use a Post-it if you need more room.)

. . . As I read on, I notice I put a star by some information because it is important . . . . Let's see if I can combine any of this when I paraphrase. (Think aloud for students so they hear how you are making the ideas your own by paraphrasing and combining ideas.)

. . . Turn and talk about what you are thinking.

. . . Do you have the idea of how you do this? Great!

. . . Remember to ask yourselves: "Can I combine ideas? Which ideas are really important? Are there questions I have? How does my background knowledge help here?"

Guide/Support Practice

TEACHING MOVES

- **Support kids to paraphrase** the information from the text in their own words.

- Offer assistance as needed, but **avoid jumping in too quickly.** When we offer too much help, we prevent kids from having the good feelings of accomplishment that come with meeting a bit of a challenge.

- **If students need more room** to paraphrase the information, they can use Post-its.

TEACHING LANGUAGE

. . . Get started. I am ready to help you if you need me. But since each of us codes according to our inner conversation, it would be super if you see what you can do first.

Wrap Up

TEACHING MOVES

- Ask students to reread their margin notes and share important information. **Make an anchor chart** to capture examples of how they used their coding to help them paraphrase and remember important information.

- **The next session** focuses on sorting out important information and interesting details.

TEACHING LANGUAGE

. . . Let's hear how it went! I'll record some of the information you thought was important.

Important Information

. . . You focused on some important information and ideas. Next time we meet, we'll sort out important information and interesting details.

ASSESS AND PLAN

Were students able to paraphrase with ease?

When we paraphrase, we not only put the author's ideas into our own words, we also omit less-important details and combine others. If kids need more support for paraphrasing, consider enlarging an information-dense paragraph and having kids cut it apart and use the important words but paraphrase the idea. If you see that a student continues to have difficulty paraphrasing, plan to confer individually and invite the student to think aloud so you can coach right at the point the student seems to have difficulty.

Check to see that students are using a variety of strategies as they code their thinking:

- asking authentic questions (including higher-level questions as well as literal questions that clarify confusions)
- paraphrasing important information in the margins
- reacting, responding, and jotting down background knowledge that furthers understanding
- clarifying and thinking through dense or confusing information

Sort Important Information and Interesting Details

In *The Comprehension Toolkit* Lesson 19, students learn to separate interesting details from information that is important to remember. This companion session for Lesson 19 gives kids more support and practice with this process, using the *Important Information/Interesting Details/My Thinking* recording form.

Companion to . . .

The Comprehension Toolkit
Lesson 19: Determine What to Remember

Text Matters

This session extends and builds on the previous two. It makes sense to use a text on which students have already coded their thinking. Readers need to have a firm grasp of the information in a text before they attempt to sift and sort important information from interesting details.

You may want to continue using the text from the previous two sessions if the text is long and full of information. Or choose a new, short article to code, and then sort the important information from the interesting details. Short texts that work well are listed in Session 18a.

Session Goals

We want students to:
- code the text (if using a new text for this session).
- distinguish between interesting details and important information.

Considerations for Planning

As kids code texts, they often think that if something is interesting *to them*, it *must be important*. In helping students distinguish between what is really important and what is just interesting, we help them build a deeper understanding of how to differentiate. Yet, we also honor the fact that interesting details make texts more engaging and memorable.

Have on hand the anchor chart of codes from Session 18a and 18b.

Students will need their own copies of the text.

Students will need copies of the recording form.

Build Background, Word and Concept Knowledge

TEACHING MOVES

- Engage kids in thinking about the **strategy of sifting and sorting** important information and interesting details as they read.

- To begin, refer back to the anchor chart of codes from Sessions 18a and 18b and **add a new code,** a wavy underline (~), to use for coding interesting details in the text. A quick review of what has gone before is essential. Students' learning accumulates and becomes richer and multidimensional as they add to their thinking repertoires.

TEACHING LANGUAGE

. . . Today we will read another text (or reread our text from the last session) that has lots of interesting information.

. . . As you know, when you read a great nonfiction text about important things, sometimes something strange or surprising captures your attention. Today we are going to learn how to sift and sort what is really important and what is just interesting. This strategy is very helpful because you'll be able to use it *forever!*

. . . To begin, let's look back at our chart of codes. Here's what I am thinking: Since we underline important information and star it, we'll put a wavy line, ~, under text that is *just interesting*. (Add the new code to the anchor chart.)

Code	Why We Coded
BK	I have background knowledge.
*	I think this is important!
?	I have a question.
R	I have a response.
_____	I underline important info.
~~	I put a wavy line under an interesting detail.

. . . Remember, interesting details catch our attention and make us want to read on. The important pieces of information are what we want to remember.

Teach/Model

- **If you are using a new text,** preview it with kids. Have them briefly share background knowledge they bring to the topic. Introduce pertinent vocabulary. Read the first paragraph and share your thinking as you code your copy of the text. Model how to code interesting details (wavy line) and important information (underline).

- **If you are using a text kids have previously coded,** model how you reread the first paragraph and make use of the margin notes and codes as you sort and sift thinking.

- Model how to **use the *Important Information/ Interesting Details/My Thinking* form.** It is provided on page 70 in *The Comprehension Toolkit* Strategy Book 5: *Determine Importance*, or you may have kids make their own forms.

- It is important for the teacher to **create a personal chart.** Modeling our own recording is important so we demonstrate how we sort and sift information and respond to it. We can merge thinking with new learning in the third column. Because we want kids to see the reading process as authentic, we open up our own thinking to them.

Important Information	Interesting Details	My Thinking

. . . Today I am going to show you how I decide what is really important and what is just interesting as I read (or reread). Let's preview the text (if using a new text). There are some words you'll need to know . . . .

. . . I'm going to begin reading (or rereading) and thinking about how my inner conversation alerts me when something is important or interesting. (Read a paragraph and think aloud as you consider what is important and what is just interesting.)

. . . This is a fascinating part here . . . . I don't think it is important, however, so I'll put a wavy line under it. But this part seems really important . . . . That gets an underline and a star! And here's what I think about this . . . . Maybe I have a question . . . or a response. I'll note that in the margins, too. (Model how you code the first paragraph.)

. . . Now I'll show you a form I'll use to record my thinking as I go. This is my *Important Information/ Interesting Details/My Thinking* form. I will paraphrase, or use my own words, because I want to write just enough to remember.

. . . I'll put the information I underlined in the *Important Information* column. I'll jot down some of the interesting details in the second column. And I'll write my responses or questions in the *My Thinking* column. Sometimes I use this column to summarize what I think are the big ideas in the text. Or I ask a lingering question.

. . . Turn and talk about what you've seen me doing.

Guide/Support Practice

- **Have kids read the text,** use the two codes as they go, and record in the columns of the *Important Information/Interesting Details/My Thinking* form.

- Move among the students and **offer support as needed.**

. . . Now it's your turn to read and do exactly what I did. Use two codes as you read: a straight underline for important information and a wavy underline for interesting details. Then use your form to record important information— what you coded with straight lines—and interesting details—what you coded with wavy lines. Remember to add your own reactions or questions in the third column.

. . . I will be around to help you, and we will have a great discussion when we finish!

Wrap Up

- **Invite kids to compare and discuss** the process, their coding, and what they wrote on their forms.

. . . What are you finding? I'll bet some of you are like me, and you had quite an inner conversation trying to decide whether something was interesting or important! Who wants to share something you coded and wrote on your form?

Assess and Plan

Did students distinguish between *important* information and *interesting* details?

If students had trouble distinguishing between *important* and *interesting*, it might be helpful to create an anchor chart showing the two terms with examples. Another option is to take examples of important information and interesting details from the text and write each example on a strip of paper or tag. Have kids sort the strips into two columns (important information/interesting details), referring back to the text to verify.

What did you notice about students' ability to sort and record on the form?

The ability to distinguish between important information and interesting details is an important skill. Pay careful attention to students who filled the second column. They may be close readers, but they may also be less able to separate important information from interesting details. Consider conferring with students individually to check their understanding and follow up with more opportunities if you find they are less confident.

Recognize the Author's Perspective

In *The Comprehension Toolkit* Lesson 20, students learn to identify and summarize the author's perspective and contrast the author's view with what they think is important in a read-aloud article. The two companion sessions for Lesson 20 break down this process. In this first session, students focus on coding what the author thinks is important with a *W*, while continuing to code what they think is important with a star.

Companion to . . .

The Comprehension Toolkit
Lesson 20: Distinguish Your Thinking
from the Author's

TEXT MATTERS

One of the most important ideas we can offer kids in reading instruction is the awareness that sometimes their own ideas of what is important in a text differ from the author's. In this session, we show students how to distinguish the writer's ideas of what is important from their own.

Texts that work well for this session have a central idea, lots of interesting details, and a clear author's perspective so that kids can distinguish this from their thinking.

A selection such as "Influential Advertising" in the *Source Book of Short Text* or "On the Move" or "Celebrating the Day of the Dead" in *Toolkit Texts: Grades 2–3* may suit your readers. These have a clear author's perspective and enough information for kids to code.

SESSION GOAL

We want students to:
- understand that what they think is important is not always the same as what the author is trying to convey.

CONSIDERATIONS FOR PLANNING

When students read nonfiction, they tend to focus on the details that make the text interesting and thought provoking. In doing so, they often miss what the writer wants them to think. We want kids to have the confidence to see their own ideas about a topic as worthy, but also to recognize that the author's purpose may be somewhat different.

Students will need to code their texts.

Build Background, Word and Concept Knowledge

- Introduce the text and **invite kids to share their ideas** about the topic. Preview vocabulary or concepts from the text that may be unfamiliar to kids.

- **Explain to students** that what a reader thinks about a text's topic is always important, but it may not be the same as the writer's ideas. Making this understanding explicit for kids is crucial. When we help students make this distinction, it frees them to be active, engaged, and passionate readers, while developing the understanding that they need to "nail" what the author is saying.

. . . I found a really interesting text for us to read today. I think you are going to like it. (Provide a specific reason why you selected the text.)

. . . I'm wondering what you know about the topic. Turn and talk for a minute. Anyone want to share your thoughts?

. . . It sounds like many of you have some ideas already. Let's talk quickly about a few words you'll need to know . . . .

. . . One of the interesting things about nonfiction is that the authors generally write because they have an interest in, and possibly strong feelings about, a topic. As we read, we may find ourselves forming a different idea from what the writer thinks is important.

. . . The reader's job is really a two-part job. We respond as readers, thinking about the interesting things we are reading, but we also think about the writer's purpose and what the writer thinks is important.

. . . It's almost as though readers have to keep a journal in their heads with two columns: one for the author's ideas and one for the reader's!

Teach/Model

- **Introduce another code** to students: *W* for *writer*. When kids use both the star to code what they think is important and the *W* to code what the author thinks, it helps them keep track of the similarities and the differences.

- **Model how you code** your copy of the text. Beginning with the title, read and think aloud about the author's important ideas and your own.

. . . Remember, we've been using codes to help us pay attention to and understand our reading.

. . . Today we will use codes again. As in the past, we will use a star when we read something really important *to us*. And we will learn a new code. When we read something we think the writer believes is important, we will code with a *W*. Now, I should tell you there will be places where we use both codes because we agree with the author.

. . . Turn and talk for a minute about what you're thinking.

. . . Let me show you how this works. I am going to read and think aloud, coding when I find something that seems really important to either the writer or me.

. . . I'm going to start with the title . . . . Almost always, the author gives us some insight about what is important in the title . . . . I am going to code the title with a *W* and a star because I think it is important, too.

. . . Now I'm going to read the first part . . . . Ah, here I think is something the writer thinks is a big idea. I will put a *W* here. (Read and code just enough so kids see what you want them to do.)

. . . Everyone see how this works? Great!

Guide/Support Practice

TEACHING MOVES	TEACHING LANGUAGE
■ **Have kids read the text,** using both the star and the *W* to distinguish thoughts about the important ideas.	. . . I want you to read on and do exactly the same as I was doing. Use the two codes, star and *W,* to help you think about the ideas.
■ Move among the students to listen in and **offer support as needed.**	. . . Remember to pay close attention to your inner conversation!
	. . . I will be around to listen in on your reading and thinking.

Wrap Up

TEACHING MOVES	TEACHING LANGUAGE
■ **Have students share their coding.** While we hope the ideas coded with a *W* are similar, ideas coded with a star may differ. Use the contrast to help kids see the difference between their views and the author's.	. . . What are you finding? Let's see. Turn, talk, and compare.
	. . . Ah, some of you found that the ideas you coded with *W* are similar, but the ideas you starred differ. What do you think that means?
■ This is a good time to mention again that readers' personal ideas are very important, but we also have to **think about the writer's purpose** and what the text is mainly about.	. . . Good thinking today! We will work some more on this when we meet next.

ASSESS AND PLAN

Were students able to note the difference between their own and the writer's important ideas?

Students may find this initial experience challenging. They really have to keep two lines of thinking open as they read. If they had difficulty, it may be worth a few extra minutes to make a quick "T chart" where you record students' thinking on one side and what they think the writer considers important on the other side. List some ideas for each side and allow time for students to engage in discussion.

> *To help children hug the shores of nonfiction, we . . . teach children to follow the main line of thought that an author puts forward.*
> (Calkins, 2001)

Companion to . . .

The Comprehension Toolkit
Lesson 20: Distinguish Your Thinking from the Author's

SESSION GOALS

We want students to:

- identify and summarize the author's perspective as well as their own.
- recognize the purpose of signal words and verbs to help bridge the background knowledge gap and make sense of reading.

Summarize the Author's Perspective

This session builds on the previous one. Using the same text, students look for signal words that indicate what the author wants the reader to remember, and then they summarize the author's perspective and contrast it with their own.

TEXT MATTERS

We continue with the text from the previous session and deepen students' understanding of how to engage with a text on a personal level. In this session, we show kids how they can watch for clues the writer leaves in the text to help them notice important ideas.

CONSIDERATIONS FOR PLANNING

Nonfiction writers generally use language skillfully. They alert readers when something really significant or surprising or unusual is about to be stated. For example, the word *surprisingly* is a signal from a writer to indicate that what is coming next is unusual or unexpected. When we teach kids to recognize the writer's clues, they often find reading to have the same enjoyment that working a puzzle involves.

In this session, we help students recognize signals the writer provides and use them to tease out important ideas, particularly when the readers have knowledge gaps. We also show kids how they can summarize the big ideas from a text, making them easier to remember.

Consider finding four or five examples of signal words or phrases authors commonly use. (See the list provided in Build Background, Word and Concept Knowledge.)

Students will need their coded texts from the previous session.

Build Background, Word and Concept Knowledge

- In this session we show students how to summarize the author's perspective. **Review the term *summarize*** and the concept of summarizing.

- Students learn to **take note of the author's signals** in nonfiction texts as they recognize the writer's words that are placed strategically to guide the reader. We have long told students to watch for signal words such as *therefore*, *first*, and *but*. What we have done less frequently is show students that when they have a gap in their background knowledge, signal words and phrases can help them infer and fill the gap.

- **Show students several examples** of signal words or phrases authors use. These often tell us the author's opinion about the information.

- **Some examples of signals:**
  If . . . , then . . .
  But . . .
  Importantly . . .
  Even after . . .
  Surprisingly . . .
  Finally . . .
  In conclusion . . .

. . . I enjoyed reading this text in our last meeting, didn't you? Who can *summarize*, or explain in a few words, what we did as we read?

. . . Right. As we read, we used two codes: a star for ideas we, the readers, think are important and a *W* for ideas we feel sure the *writer* thinks are important.

. . . Does anyone want to share your thoughts about how that went?

. . . Today we will look back through our reading for something really important. Do you know that writers, especially in nonfiction, offer us signals to help us as readers?

. . . Let me show you. (Show some examples of signals.) Let's look at these examples to see how the writer is often a great help in alerting us to what is important.

. . . Today we will reread to look for signals in the text, and then we'll see how we can summarize the writer's important ideas.

Teach/Model

■ **Use your own coded text** to demonstrate how the students will look through their text to reassess their coding and circle signal words that note important ideas.

■ Then, skimming those coded ideas, **show kids how you write a summary** of what matters most to you, the reader, and then what matters most to the writer. Finally, show how to write a comparison of the two perspectives.

. . . Let's look back through our coding. I am going to reread quickly to see if I find any signal words where I marked the text with a *W.* Ah, here is a signal word. The text says . . . , and I do have a star there. I'm going to circle any of those signal words or phrases I find.

. . . Turn and talk for a minute about how you think rereading like this might help you find the writer's key or main ideas.

. . . Let me reread a little more. (Model just enough to be sure kids know what to do.)

. . . Once I look back over my coding, and by the way, I may code a few more things as I reread, I am going to flip my text so I can write on the back of it.

. . . First I'm gong to write what *I* thought was most important. (Model writing a summary statement that connects the ideas you starred as most important.) Then I'll draw a line. Under the line, I will write what I think the author thought was most important. Finally (and did you hear that signal word?), I will write a comparison of the two statements.

. . . Does everyone see how this works? What I am doing is using my coding to help me determine the big ideas in the text.

Guide/Support Practice

TEACHING MOVES

- **Have kids reread the text,** noting where they coded using stars and *W*s. Have them circle any signal words the author uses.

- Have kids **use their coding to summarize** what they think is important and what they believe the author considers most important.

- As students work, you may want to **list signal words and phrases** they find.

TEACHING LANGUAGE

. . . I want you to read on and do exactly the same as I was doing. Use the two codes to help you think about the ideas. Look for signals the writer uses and circle them.

. . . Then, when you have done that, flip your paper over and write what you think is important, draw a line, and then write what you think the author thinks. Remember, it could be almost the same, it could be similar, or it might be different. When you have written the two, draw another line and compare them. There's no wrong or right here!

. . . I will be here to help you.

Wrap Up

TEACHING MOVES

- **Have students turn and talk,** comparing what they wrote and how alike or different the two statements may be.

TEACHING LANGUAGE

. . . Let's turn and talk about what we wrote.

. . . Do you see that this is really helpful? If we can consider our own and the author's thinking as two ways of looking at a text, then we will find it easier to understand. All of us read based on what we know. *Now* we know something new! Sometimes the author and the reader agree and sometimes they don't. But both lines of thinking matter!

ASSESS AND PLAN

Were students able to summarize the author's key ideas?

Helping kids recognize the two lines of thinking readers use as they read (thinking about the author's perspective and their own) enriches their inner conversation. For too many years, we have focused solely on finding the main idea, thereby ignoring the reader's concerns. Both matter. This may seem a bit confusing to kids at first. If it does, offer a variety of articles they can use to practice the process again. Then collect their work to see where they might need more coaching.

Use a *Topic/Detail/ Response* Chart

In *The Comprehension Toolkit* Lesson 21, students create a *Topic/Detail/ Response (TDR)* chart to sift through and combine supporting details to come up with big ideas in a read-aloud article. This companion session for Lesson 21 gives students more support and practice using a *TDR* chart as they read another text.

Companion to . . .

The Comprehension Toolkit
Lesson 21: Construct Main Ideas
from Supporting Details

TEXT MATTERS

The *Topic/Detail/Response* chart is perfect for texts divided by subheads. This text structure matches up well and supports kids in their initial experience with the chart. Sections punctuated with subheads provide a scaffold, helping kids see that the heading, whether standard or inferential, is the larger topic and what follows are the details.

Short texts that have subheads include "Animal Helpers" and "Wings in the Water" in *Toolkit Texts: Grades 2–3* and "Racing for Life" in the *Source Book of Short Text.* Consider, too, using one of the many non-fiction tradebooks organized with subheads.

CONSIDERATIONS FOR PLANNING

The *Topic/Detail/Response* chart is an excellent way to help students read in the content areas. When students use tools such as the *TDR* chart, they develop strategies to manage information that may at first seem overwhelming. By using the *TDR* chart, students have a way to classify information so they can see relationships among bits of information. Kids find that using the chart increases their understanding and engagement because as they read they are thinking about how parts fit into the whole.

Students will need individual *Topic/Detail/Response* charts.

SESSION GOALS

We want students to:

- begin to use the *Topic/ Detail/Response* chart to distinguish details from the bigger ideas in the text.
- understand and articulate how the details support and develop the larger topic or idea.

Build Background, Word and Concept Knowledge

■ **Introduce the text** to kids and build engagement through activating their background knowledge. Building on their previous work with standard and inferential subheads (Session 13), preview the text.

■ **Preview pertinent vocabulary** or concepts kids will need to know.

■ **Introduce the *TDR* chart.** You can use the *TDR* form on page 71 in *The Comprehension Toolkit* Strategy Book 5: *Determine Importance*, or have students make their own chart with three columns labeled *Topic*, *Detail*, and *Response*.

. . . I think you'll enjoy reading the text I have selected. And I know you'll find the chart we'll learn to use very helpful.

. . . Take a moment to look through the text. What are you noticing?

. . . Right! The author organizes the article around subheads. When we talked about this text feature before, we learned there are two kinds of subheads. Who remembers one? (Help kids recall the two types—standard and inferential—and what characterizes each.)

. . . Turn and talk about something you think you'll learn in this text, and share a question you are already wondering.

. . . Let's talk about some words you'll need to know . . . .

. . . Now, here's the chart I mentioned. I call it a *thinksheet* because that is what it is! It helps us with our thinking.

. . . It has three columns, and we call it a *Topic/ Detail/Response* chart. Here's how we will use it. We'll write big topics in the first column, and record details that go with the big ideas in the second column. There's a third column for our responses. What I love about this thinksheet is it helps me organize my thinking as I'm reading.

Topic	Detail	Response

Teach/Model

- **Begin to read and model** how to use the *TDR* chart. When kids discover how text structure and note taking can help them as readers, they develop a sense of agency— an "I can" spirit.

- The teacher's careful model does two things in this session. It demystifies nonfiction by **showing how subheads act as guideposts** through the text, **and the chart becomes an organizer** on which kids can see the relationships between big ideas and supporting details.

- **Offering a place to record responses** heightens kids' awareness of their inner conversation.

. . . I'm going to begin reading this article. You follow along. As I read, I will share my thinking and model how I use the *TDR* chart.

. . . As I read the title . . . I notice I have an idea what the author is writing about.

. . . Turn and talk about what you're thinking.

. . . As I read on, I'm noticing the way the author helps me by including subheads. I find those really helpful because they guide my reading and tell me what that particular section will be about. That's the *topic!*

. . . I will stop at this subhead . . . and record what this section will be about in the *Topic* column. Since this is a subhead, I think the writer will give me some details about this topic as I read the section.

. . . (Read on.) Wow! This is an interesting detail. I'll record it in the *Detail* column. Then in the *Response* column I'll record that I find this so surprising. I write my reactions and responses in this column.

. . . So you see how we use the text feature— subheads—in combination with this *TDR* think-sheet. Very cool, right?

Guide/Support Practice

TEACHING MOVES

- After ensuring that students know what to do, **have them read on and record** information on their *TDR* charts.

- Move among the students to listen in and **offer support as needed.**

TEACHING LANGUAGE

. . . I want you to read on now and do exactly as I was doing. Use the subheads to guide you, and think about how the details relate to and support the larger topics.

. . . Listen to your inner conversation for responses. Who can tell me some things your inner voice might say?

. . . I will be around to listen in on your reading and help if you have questions about the *TDR* chart.

Wrap Up

TEACHING MOVES

- Guide kids to **share what they learned.** Help students notice and name what they've done. One of the important ways we support kids is by helping them see how purposeful actions make their reading more productive.

TEACHING LANGUAGE

. . . What did you learn as you read? Let's think about the text in sections, the way the author wrote it. Who wants to share something you learned— first the topic and then the details?

. . . We talk a lot in school about main ideas and details. It often seems challenging to pick out the main ideas, but using a *TDR* chart to work strategically really helps, doesn't it?

. . . Try using a *TDR* chart when you're reading your textbooks or other nonfiction books.

ASSESS AND PLAN

Did students seem confident as they recorded the topics and supporting details?

If some students had difficulty seeing the relationships between the topics and supporting details, you may want to create a different arrangement to assist them. Consider making a chart that organizes details and responses under each topic. Just seeing the chart organized in a slightly different way may help some students.

Topic	Topic	Topic
Details	Details	Details
Response	Response	Response

Determine Importance

After this unit, you want to know that students are sorting and sifting information to remember the most important ideas, so your conference should help the student use several different approaches to determining importance.

1. **Invite the student to choose a passage and create a context for it.**
   - Choose a part of your book to read to me.
   - Tell me what it's about.
   - Tell me about the most important ideas in this text.

2. **Focus on how the student organizes his or her thinking to determine what is important to remember.**
   - What helped you to determine what was important to remember as you read? Share some interesting details with me. Talk about how you sifted out what was important from what was interesting.
   - Did you learn anything new (facts) as you read this? What do you wonder (questions) about this new information? What are your reactions and responses to this information?
   - What would you write in your notes on this section? How would your notes help you understand and remember?
   - Was there a place in the text that was hard to understand? How did you sort and sift the information to better understand the text?

3. **Ask the student to distinguish between what she or he thinks is important to remember and what the author wants readers to remember.**
   - Share something in the text that you think is important to remember.
   - Now tell me about something that the author wants you to remember from this article/piece.
   - Was there a place where your perspective (or opinion if appropriate) on this topic is very different from the author's? Tell me about that.

Reading Conference Recording Form: Determine Importance	
Name _____ Date _____	
Book title _____	
GOAL	**EVIDENCE**
The student . . .	This student . . .
1. Understands the text • Tells what the book is about and what she or he learned by reading it	
2. Describes how he or she sifts interesting details from important information • Explains how facts, questions, and responses supported learning new information • Tells how note-taking scaffolds, coding the text, and margin notes help sort and sift information	
3. Distinguishes between the reader's thinking and the author's thinking • Notes the difference between what he or she wants to remember and what the author thinks is important • Discerns the difference between her or his own perspective and the author's perspective or opinions	

©2010 by Stephanie Harvey, Anne Goudvis, and Judy Wallis. From *Comprehension Intervention: Small-Group Lessons for The Comprehension Toolkit*. Portsmouth, NH: Heinemann. This page may be copied for classroom use only.

Conference Recording Form for "Determine Importance," located in "Resources" section.

Follow-Ups

If the student has difficulty with any of the primary goals in this unit, prompts like the following may be helpful during independent work in subsequent units.

- Tell me about the important information.
- Share any questions or responses you have to this information.
- Did you keep the difference between interesting details and important information in mind as you read?
- Did you discern the difference between what you think is important to remember and what the author thought was most important?

Language students may use
to demonstrate that they are distinguishing important ideas

- This is important to remember.
- I think the big idea is . . .
- The author thinks . . . is important to remember, but what I think is important is . . .
- This is really interesting information, but what seems to be most important is . . .

Summarize and Synthesize

Synthesizing information nudges readers to see the bigger picture as they read. It's not enough for readers simply to recall or restate the facts. Thoughtful readers integrate the new information with their existing knowledge to come to a more complete understanding of the text and of the subject.

As readers encounter new information, their thinking evolves. They merge new information with what they already know and construct meaning as they go. As they distill nonfiction text into a few important ideas, they may develop a new perspective or an original insight.

Take Notes, Paraphrase, and Respond

In *The Comprehension Toolkit* Lesson 22, students learn strategies for navigating challenging text, taking notes, and responding to information. They record important information, paraphrase and respond to it, and monitor their understanding as they react to a read-aloud article. This companion session offers students more support and practice with these strategies as they read another text and use a *Notes/Thinking* chart.

Companion to . . .

The Comprehension Toolkit
Lesson 22: Read, Think, and React

TEXT MATTERS

Texts that have subheads help kids learn to "chunk" information. When we use texts that have subheads, kids learn not only to depend on the text structure to assist them, but also that summarizing is as much a "during reading" process as an "after reading" activity.

A short article with headings works well for this session. "Ozone Hole," "Tigers Roar Back," and "A Focus on Girls' Education" in the *Source Book of Short Text*, and "Animal Ears" in *Toolkit Texts: Grades 2–3* have subheads that will help kids navigate the text, take notes, and monitor their understanding as they read.

CONSIDERATIONS FOR PLANNING

We show kids that summarizing is how we think about and react to text. When students see that reading is an active, rather than passive, process, they learn to respond to the text and information as they read. Paraphrasing encourages kids to merge their background knowledge with what they are reading in the text.

In this session, we focus on the process of summarizing and offer students a way to record information using the *Notes/Thinking* chart.

Students will need individual *Notes/Thinking* forms.

SESSION GOALS

We want students to:

- pull out important information that relates to key ideas and paraphrase it.
- learn strategies for navigating challenging text, taking notes, and responding to the information.
- monitor their understanding as they read.

Build Background, Word and Concept Knowledge

- **Preview the text together.** Help students activate their prior knowledge about the topic. Discuss the meaning of any unfamiliar words or concepts to facilitate reading. Encourage students to share what they wonder. The questions kids ask as they preview often help them tackle the text in a more active way. Reading to answer authentic questions increases engagement.

- **Introduce the *Notes/Thinking* form.** You can find this form on page 63 of *The Comprehension Toolkit* Strategy Book 6: *Summarize and Synthesize*, or have students make their own chart with two columns and the headings *Notes* and *Thinking*.

- **Review the terms *paraphrasing* and *summarizing*** as they come up in the session.

. . . Let's look at the article I brought today. It is so interesting! (Connect kids to the topic.)

. . . Turn and talk about what you notice and your background knowledge about the topic.

. . . Who wants to share some of what you noticed or your own knowledge about the topic?

. . . Let's talk about some vocabulary you'll need to know.

. . . It sounds as though you are wondering about some things as well as noticing some interesting information you found as you previewed.

. . . I want to share a form we will use today. It's a note-taking form designed to help you gather information as you read. (Give kids the *Notes/Thinking* form or have them create their own.)

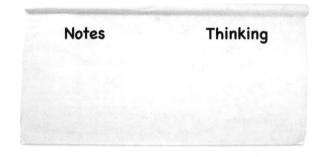

. . . As we read, we will think about the information we are reading and jot it down—take notes—in the *Notes* column.

. . . As you write important information, put it in your own words. Remember, we call that *paraphrasing*. When we can explain something in our own words, we really understand it!

. . . The second column, *Thinking*, is where you will record your questions and reactions to what you are reading.

Teach/Model

- **Begin to read and model** the note-taking process. Teach kids to think about the topic and then how to summarize as they read.

- In the demonstration, **show kids how you record,** paraphrase, activate your own background knowledge (*BK*), and record questions you hope the text will answer.

- As you read and model for students, **talk through what you will write** in the *Notes* column first, then jot it down and record your reactions and questions in the *Thinking* column. Summarizing and paraphrasing orally is an important first step in helping kids record successfully.

> **Teaching Tip**
> When we summarize, we often shorten key ideas into our own words. By shortening ideas and paraphrasing them, we show kids how summarizing and paraphrasing aid understanding. Having kids summarize orally before they do so in writing eases the task for them.

. . . Let me begin to read the text and show you how this note-taking process works. (Read part of the text.)

. . . That is pretty interesting. I am going to tell you what I just learned and then write the information in my *Notes* column. (Paraphrase orally; then record.) I also have a question about what I read, so I will jot it in my *Thinking* column. If I use my background knowledge, I will code it as *BK*. (Read and model several examples so kids see what you want them to do.)

. . . Turn and talk about what you see me doing.

. . . So, now I have some important information paraphrased in the *Notes* column, and I have some reactions and questions recorded in my *Thinking* column.

. . . Notice that I didn't write complete sentences—I just wrote words and phrases to capture the main information.

. . . Let's read a little more. (Read another short section.) I'll stop here. Turn and talk about how you'd paraphrase what we just read.

Guide/Support Practice

- **Ask students to summarize** what they are going to do. Make sure kids understand the process of taking notes and recording their thinking.

- Remind kids to **try paraphrasing orally** before they write. Some students may have difficulty paraphrasing the author's words. Paraphrasing and using short phrases to capture ideas and information can be challenging. One way to support kids is to have them paraphrase orally first and then jot their notes.

- Move among the students and listen in to their reading and recording. **Offer support as needed.**

. . . Now it's your turn. Who can *summarize*—or tell us in a few words—what we're going to do?

. . . Great! One strategy to try is thinking through how you will paraphrase the information in your head before you write it. Or you can turn and talk with someone next to you—talk about what you are going to write in your *Notes* column. Be sure to merge your own thinking with the new information you are learning.

. . . When you are using your background knowledge, add the abbreviation *BK* to code it.

. . . And remember, write the information in short phrases, not long sentences!

. . . I will be around to listen and help you.

Wrap Up

- **Have kids share** what they wrote on their *Notes/Thinking* charts.

- **Make an anchor chart** with kids to help them think of all the strategies they used to navigate the text and make notes. Be sure to prompt for things you'd like students to remember.

. . . Great! I see you've written important information in the *Notes* column and your own thoughts about that information in the *Thinking* column.

. . . Let's share our learning and our thinking. Turn and talk about what you wrote in the *Notes* column, and share your thinking as well.

. . . I see you merged your own background knowledge because you recorded a *BK* beside what you knew.

. . . Let's think of some of the strategies you used as you read and make an anchor chart to help us remember what we can do.

How to Take Notes in Challenging Texts

- Say the information out loud before writing it to practice paraphrasing.
- Record your reactions and questions in the "Thinking" column.
- Use the subheads to help you think about the important information and organize it.

ASSESS AND PLAN

Did some students have trouble putting the text's ideas into their own words?

Students may need additional modeling and coaching as they begin to use paraphrasing. To make the process visual for kids, consider making a copy of the text and actually "cutting out" the important words and ideas. Arranging these into a phrase makes the paraphrasing process tangible and helps kids understand it more clearly.

> *Reading and thinking are invisible, but I can create some structures that help me see what's going on in my students' heads.* (Serravallo and Goldberg, 2007)

Extend and Expand Your Thinking

In *The Comprehension Toolkit* Lesson 23, students focus on extending and expanding their thinking as they respond to a read-aloud article. They synthesize facts, consider larger issues and ideas, and share their thinking on a class chart. This companion session offers students the opportunity to practice thinking beyond the text as they read another article.

Companion to . . .

The Comprehension Toolkit
Lesson 23: Think Beyond the Text

TEXT MATTERS

Select a text that will expand kids' thinking, promote questions, and invite inferences.

A short article with powerful ideas works well, such as "Women of the Negro Leagues" in *Toolkit Texts: Grades 4–5* or "All Aboard the Underground Railroad" in *Toolkit Texts: Grades 6–7*. These allow kids to surface their prior knowledge and synthesize new information into bigger ideas. A more challenging choice is "Storm Surge" in *Toolkit Texts: Grades 6–7.* "From Egg to Salamander" and "Rock Secrets" in *Toolkit Texts: Grades 2–3* also provide enough information to expand and extend kids' knowledge.

CONSIDERATIONS FOR PLANNING

In this session, we support readers in going beyond facts and details to inferring bigger ideas. When readers use their background knowledge *together* with the facts and details, they are able to surface the larger ideas. Through both questions and inferences, readers use their inner conversation to draw conclusions that move them beyond the literal information to rich, new learning.

You will need small Post-its to mark the text and larger Post-its or pieces of paper for the "big" ideas.

Students will need Post-its.

SESSION GOALS

We want students to:

- respond to the information with questions, connections, and inferences that expand their thinking.
- synthesize the facts and draw conclusions to consider larger issues and ideas.
- make their thinking visible and learn from each other as they share responses, questions, and ideas.

Build Background, Word and Concept Knowledge

TEACHING MOVES

- Help kids **activate their background knowledge.** We want them to use it to expand their thinking. In this session, we have kids use Post-its to jot down big ideas and questions they wonder about as they read. Sometimes a concrete example helps, so we use small Post-its to leave tracks of our thinking in the text. We use larger Post-its or pieces of paper to jot down the bigger ideas in the wrap-up discussion.

- **Preview the text with kids.** Invite them to briefly share their background knowledge. Introduce words or concepts that may be unfamiliar.

TEACHING LANGUAGE

. . . You've had lots of experiences using Post-its to leave tracks of your thinking as you read. Today we will use Post-its to think about the big ideas in the text.

. . . You've all seen how thoughtful questions asked during our reading prompt new learning.

. . . Today you'll see how our ideas grow out of our reading, combining and connecting to our own background knowledge.

. . . Let's preview the text together. Turn and talk about what you notice.

. . . What do you already know about this topic?

. . . Here are some words that may be new to you . . .

Teach/Model

■ **Begin reading and modeling.** Show students how you record facts, questions, and bigger issues and ideas on Post-its.

■ **Invite kids to participate with their ideas.** We want students to reflect on a topic and see not only what is in the text, but also how to go beyond the text by questioning and inferring.

. . . I'm going to begin reading the text, and I'll think aloud as I go to show you how I get to even bigger ideas than those explicitly stated in the text. It's like I'm "collecting" the facts and information in the article to arrive at a big idea.

. . . I'm going to record these facts on my Post-its.

. . . As I read on, I think about what the information may mean in a larger sense. For example, when I read about . . . , I am also thinking about and wondering what that means beyond the information I've written down. (Use examples from the text to show kids that although you use the textual information, you also consider bigger issues and ideas that you can conclude by merging your thinking with the information. Guide the kids to participate and weigh in with their ideas. In this way they experience how we often arrive at big ideas through discussion.)

. . . Turn and talk about what you see me doing.

Guide/Support Practice

TEACHING MOVES

- **Have students read** and record their thinking on Post-its.

- **Confer with kids as they are reading.** Note if they understand how the information in the text connects to larger ideas.

TEACHING LANGUAGE

. . . I want you to read on and put your own facts, questions, and inferences on your Post-its. Remember that your inner conversation will nudge you to bigger ideas.

. . . Remember, we are thinking beyond this text to bigger ideas. The facts in the text are like a bridge you cross to get to the bigger ideas and issues.

. . . When you finish reading, we will consider all our ideas to see how they connect. That will be a perfect time to share out our thinking and discuss the big ideas together.

. . . I will be around to listen and help you.

Wrap Up

TEACHING MOVES

- **Have kids compare their Post-its** and consider how they moved beyond the text to bigger ideas. Because we are asking students to think beyond the text, kids may arrive at different conclusions. This may encourage good discussion.

- **Record the bigger ideas** on bigger Post-its or pieces of paper.

Teaching Tip

If you have access to a poster maker, consider making an enlarged copy of the text that you can lay out on a table or the floor. Have students remove their individual Post-its and place them in the same part of the group text.

TEACHING LANGUAGE

. . . I see that you have Post-its on your own text. Let's put all of our Post-its on one copy of the text and see if we can summarize our thinking as a group.

. . . Let's look over our Post-its and use them to summarize the big ideas and conclusions we can draw. (Help students think about the ideas written on their Post-its.) What big ideas do you see? (Jot these on bigger Post-its or pieces of paper to make your point.)

. . . Good thinking! Notice how we began with all these facts and built on them to get to the bigger ideas. Sometimes we have lingering questions as well, and those can lead us on to further reading and learning.

ASSESS AND PLAN

Were students able to move beyond the literal level of the text to the larger ideas?

Drawing conclusions from text and synthesizing factual information to get to larger ideas and implications is challenging for kids. Use thought-provoking read-aloud selections as a way to support students as they move toward more sophisticated thinking.

Check to make sure students are incorporating strategies as tools and that they are able to use "strategy language" to share thinking:
- asking authentic questions to extend their thinking
- inferring and drawing conclusions about the information

Language to look for: "The big idea here is . . ."; "One new idea I had was . . ."; "In conclusion . . . ." See page 61 in *The Comprehension Toolkit* Strategy Book 6: *Summarize and Synthesize* for additional language stems that illustrate summarizing and synthesizing.

Synthesizing information nudges us to see the bigger picture . . . . Thoughtful readers merge their thinking with the information to come to a more complete under-standing of the text and the topic. (Guthrie, Wigfield, and Perencevich, 2004)

Companion to . . .

The Comprehension Toolkit
Lesson 24: Read to Get the Gist

Session Goal

We want students to:

■ slow down and think about the text, separating the ancillary details from the bigger ideas to get the gist.

Pull Out the Big Ideas

In *The Comprehension Toolkit* Lesson 24, students learn to reduce information to a manageable amount by pulling out the big ideas, summarizing the big picture, and responding to a read-aloud article. The two companion sessions for Lesson 24 offer students more support and practice with this process. In this first session, students focus on pulling out the big ideas as they read a selected text.

Text Matters

Select a text organized by subheads. The natural divisions created by the author offer students chunks that make the text more accessible to summarize. It is better to select a text that is slightly too easy, rather than too difficult.

"Navaho Code Talkers" and "All Wrapped Up" in *Toolkit Texts: Grades 4–5*, "What's Your Type?" and "The Greenhouse Effect" in the *Source Book of Short Text*, and "Animal Helpers" in *Toolkit Texts: Grades 2–3* are divided into sections that scaffold readers' efforts to summarize and capture the gist of the text.

Considerations for Planning

By offering kids multiple opportunities to tackle nonfiction texts, we help them gain experience and familiarity with text structures and organizational patterns. Just as readers come to expect a story to be organized in a series of episodes, so students become more agile in using nonfiction structures that alert readers to important infor-mation, key ideas, and shifts in topics.

In this session, we help kids slow down their reading, become more selective in gathering information, and increase their awareness of the bigger, more important ideas. In the next session, we help them sort and keep only the big ideas. When we support kids in reading for gist, we show them how to use questions, connections, and inferences to enhance understanding.

Students will need Post-its.

Build Background, Word and Concept Knowledge

- **Help kids activate prior knowledge.** This remains a priority in our instruction. We continue to show our students that though their depth of background knowledge may be limited, it always serves them well to consider it as they begin to read.

- **Introduce the terms *gist* and *synthesize*.** Offer examples that help kids understand the concepts of gist and synthesis.

. . . I love learning new words, don't you? Words often stand for big ideas. Here's a word I think you'll enjoy learning: *gist*. *Gist* means "the central or main idea."

. . . We often use the word *gist* when we are talking about nonfiction texts because informational texts can have lots and lots of details. We can't—and we don't want to—remember all these details, so we read with the goal of finding the gist in the reading. So we read, pare down the information, and just focus on a big idea.

. . . I sometimes think nonfiction reading is like making stew. We use all sorts of good stuff to make stew, including lots of liquid. But we boil down the stew until much of the liquid is gone. What we have left is like the gist—the most important parts. All the things we added give our stew flavor, just like the details a writer adds, but in the end, they are *synthesized* into the most important part. (Consider using your own analogy here—something that helps kids understand how we synthesize when we read for gist.)

. . . When we *synthesize*, we don't have to tell every detail; we focus on just the most important parts. So, if we were to synthesize our school day yesterday, we wouldn't have to tell everything we did in great detail. We would just think about the important things that occurred in the day.

Teach/Model

- **Preview the text with kids.** Ask them to briefly share what they know about the topic. Introduce vocabulary or concepts that may be unfamiliar.

- **Point out the subheads** in the text and review the two types, *standard* and *inferential*.

- **Read the first section and model how you record the gist of the section on a Post-it.** Orally rehearse before recording. Demonstrate how you paraphrase and summarize to record the gist. In this session, we want kids to note important ideas or the gist in each of the text's sections. In the next session, we will help them sift and sort which ideas are most important.

. . . Today we are going to read a really interesting article, and we will use Post-its to track our thinking as we read.

. . . Let's preview the text. Turn and talk about what you notice. What do you already know about the topic?

. . . Here are some words that may be new to you . . .

. . . Did you notice that the text is divided into sections? Who remembers what we call those headings and how we use them as readers? Right! They are called subheads, and there are two kinds . . . (prompt kids to remember *standard* and *inferential*). As readers, we use the subheads to help us know or infer what is coming in that section.

. . . I'll start reading, and as I read I'm going to record the gist of each section on a Post-it.

. . . Notice how I read just this section. I'll put the information in my own words and say just what's most important, and then I'll jot it down on my Post-it.

. . . Turn and talk about what you see me doing.

Guide/Support Practice

TEACHING MOVES

- **Do a section together** to be sure students understand.

- **As kids read on,** move among them and note what they are writing on their Post-its.

- **If you sense kids are struggling** with recognizing important ideas, offer support. Using the analogy of "heavy" and "light" ideas, have kids visualize holding the ideas in their hands and "weighing" them before writing the "heaviest," or most important, ideas on the Post-its.

TEACHING LANGUAGE

. . . Let's do another section together. (Discuss important information and jot it down together.)

. . . Now it's your turn to read on and record important ideas on Post-its. Listen to your inner conversation!

. . . I will be around to listen and help you.

Wrap Up

TEACHING MOVES

- **Invite kids to share their Post-its.** In the following session, you'll engage kids in sorting their ideas into two categories: *Is a BIG Idea/ Is NOT a Big Idea.*

- **For the next session,** students will need their texts marked with Post-its.

TEACHING LANGUAGE

. . . I see you've written lots of Post-its! Let's share what we recorded.

. . . When we meet again, we will sort through our Post-its to decide which are the most important ideas. Remember, we want to synthesize our ideas to get the "gist" of what's happening in the article. Good work today!

ASSESS AND PLAN

Were students selective in their use of Post-its, using them to mark the biggest ideas in each section?

If readers put many Post-its on the text, it may be an indication that they are less confident in discriminating which ideas are the important ones. In the next session, you'll have an opportunity to think aloud and model the sifting process.

Pare Down and Synthesize Ideas

This session builds on the previous one. Students consider the ideas they have pulled from the text, pare them down, and synthesize further to get the gist of the article.

Companion to ...

The Comprehension Toolkit
Lesson 24: Read to Get the Gist

TEXT MATTERS

Continue with the text used in the previous session.

CONSIDERATIONS FOR PLANNING

In the previous session, we asked students to record on Post-its the most important ideas—the *gist*—of each section of the article.

In this session, we help kids sort their Post-its, checking to be sure they've captured the big ideas. Students see that synthesizing is about going to the very essence of meaning. We want kids to learn how to think about the text, find the gist, and still understand the importance of their own connections, questions, and inferences formed as they read.

Decide how you will prepare the three circles kids will use to sort their Post-its. You may want to have kids create the circles with you.

Students will need their texts with Post-its from the previous session.

SESSION GOALS

We want students to:

- slow down and think about the text, separating the ancillary details from the bigger ideas to get the gist.

- synthesize the facts and draw conclusions to consider larger issues and ideas.

- make their thinking visible and learn from each other as they share responses, questions, and ideas.

Build Background, Word and Concept Knowledge

TEACHING MOVES

- **Review the term** *gist* that kids learned in the previous session. Remind them that as they read the article, they wrote the gist of each section on Post-its.

TEACHING LANGUAGE

. . . We talked about some important ideas when we last met. Who remembers the word we use when we're talking about capturing the most important ideas in a text?

. . . Right! *Gist* is when we delete the less important parts and synthesize the most important parts. In our last session, you wrote the gist of each section on Post-its as you read the text.

Teach/Model

TEACHING MOVES

- **Have kids revisit the text** and their Post-its, rereading quickly with this question in mind: "Are the ideas I wrote the *most important* in this section of the text?" In this session, we help kids sift and sort which ideas are most important.

- **Ask kids to share and discuss their Post-its,** considering how they capture the gist of a particular section.

TEACHING LANGUAGE

. . . Today we're going to review what we wrote and sort out the most important ideas.

. . . First, quickly reread the text and your Post-its. Ask yourself: "Are the ideas I wrote the *most important* in this section of the text?"

. . . Turn and talk about what you wrote. Compare how you captured the gist of each section.

Guide/Support Practice

TEACHING MOVES

- **Have kids star the Post-its** they believe capture the big ideas.

- **Help students sort their ideas.** Explain that you've created three circles for kids to use for sorting their Post-its: *Is a BIG Idea, Is NOT a Big Idea,* and *Not Sure.* Consider using a large piece of butcher paper and preparing the circles with the kids.

TEACHING LANGUAGE

. . . Now that you've had a chance to reread, star the Post-its you think *really* capture the big idea or gist of each section.

. . . Great! Now we are going to sort our Post-its. I have three circles: One says *Is a BIG Idea,* and another says *Is NOT a Big Idea.* The third circle says *Not Sure.*

. . . Let's sort our Post-its into these three categories. Here's the rule, however. Only *one* of your Post-its can go in the *Not Sure* circle!

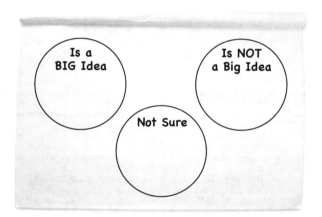

Wrap Up

TEACHING MOVES

- Have students **look for duplicate ideas** and select the Post-it with the best wording. Playing "Post-it Note Survival" is a great way to help kids make qualitative decisions about wording.

- **Ask kids** if some Post-its can be combined, and help them think about how to do so.

- When students have pared down to the gist, ask them to **share their own thinking** about the article.

TEACHING LANGUAGE

. . . You've categorized your Post-its. Does anyone see one you think is a duplicate idea?

. . . Can we combine some Post-its into one idea?

. . . Now we are down to just a few key ideas that are related, aren't we? These ideas are the gist of the article!

. . . Turn and talk about your own thinking about this text. What questions, connections, or inferences do you have? Sharing your own thinking is important!

ASSESS AND PLAN

Did some students struggle when they were asked to categorize and sort out key ideas?

Since summarizing and synthesizing are as much about deleting as they are about keeping ideas, it is helpful for kids to go through this process more than once. Offering kids additional practice in short articles that have subheads is an ideal way to support learning. For more articles with subheads, see *Toolkit Texts* for your readers' level.

Companion to . . .

The Comprehension Toolkit
Lesson 25: Reread and Rethink

Distinguish Between Facts and Opinions

In *The Comprehension Toolkit* Lesson 25, students monitor their understanding of what they've read in a read-aloud article. They check facts and information and correct their misunderstandings so their opinions are based on solid evidence from the text. The two companion sessions for Lesson 25 offer kids more support and practice with this process. In this first session, they focus on the difference between facts and opinions.

TEXT MATTERS

Select a text that will evoke students' responses, questions, and opinions. A text that deals with current issues will stir kids' responses and give them opportunities to tease out facts from the opinions.

A short, evocative article works well, such as "War" in *Toolkit Texts: Grades 4–5* or "The Importance of Hard Work," an article about Wilma Rudolph, in the *Source Book of Short Text*. "Moon Walking" and "Fossils" in *Toolkit Texts: Grades 2–3* also lend themselves to distinguishing between facts and opinions.

SESSION GOAL

We want students to:
- understand the difference between facts and opinions.

CONSIDERATIONS FOR PLANNING

In this session, we show students how our thinking evolves as we read. In our modeling, we demonstrate how we change our ideas upon encountering new information in a text. We help kids see that, while their opinions matter, to gain the essence of a text they must find evidence to support or revise their opinions. Reading to consider how personal opinions and ideas might need revising helps students proceed in a responsible as well as engaged way.

Students will need Post-its for this session.

Build Background, Word and Concept Knowledge

- **Review the terms** *facts* **and** *opinions*. Make sure kids can explain the difference.

- **Our goal in this session** is to help kids separate out the facts from their own opinions. Sometimes students read with their own opinions in control, rather than reading with openness to ideas and information presented in the text. We value kids' opinions because they are merging their own thinking with the information in the text. But we know opinions can obscure accurate information, so we also encourage kids to suspend their judgments and opinions so they are open to learning new information.

. . . We all have opinions on many things. We form our opinions generally out of our own thinking and experiences. When we read, we know our thinking matters. But we must also look for evidence in the text to support our ideas.

. . . Two words are important here: *facts* and *opinions.*

. . . What is a *fact?* Right! Something that is true.

. . . And an *opinion?* Exactly! It is our own viewpoint or perspective.

. . . We'll learn that both facts and opinions are important and we use both to become thoughtful, critical readers.

Teach/Model

- Begin reading the text. Model how you **record facts and your opinions** and code them on Post-its as you read.

. . . As we read the article, we will track our thinking. I'll read the first part to you and share my thinking about both the information and my responses to and opinions about that information. (Read a short section.)

. . . Here is a fact. The author says . . . I will jot that down on a Post-it and code it with an *F* for *fact.*

. . . I have an opinion . . . . Sometimes that can be my reaction to that fact. I will record my opinion here on a Post-it and code it with an *O.*

. . . So I'm thinking . . . . That's my opinion. But wait a minute; here it says . . . . So now I have some additional information. This changes my thinking. Now I think . . . . (Record and code facts and opinions on Post-its.)

Guide/Support Practice

TEACHING MOVES

- **Have students read** the text and record facts and their opinions on Post-its. Though kids may not revise their thinking until the next session, here we want them to read with a greater awareness of their own opinions and the facts the author presents.

TEACHING LANGUAGE

. . . Now you read, recording important facts and what you think about them—your opinions. Remember to code your Post-its with *F* for *facts* and *O* for your *opinions*.

. . . I will be around to listen and help you.

Wrap Up

TEACHING MOVES

- **Ask students to share** their experience of recording facts and opinions. While we hope students will see their own thinking evolving, we save that explicit teaching about the evolution of thought until the next session.

- **For the next session,** students will need their texts and their Post-its.

TEACHING LANGUAGE

. . . I can see you worked hard reading and recording! I noticed you recorded facts, or information, and you reacted and responded with your thoughts about the information—your opinions.

. . . Who wants to share a fact you recorded? Who wants to share an opinion?

. . . Now that you have your Post-its coded with an *F* or an *O*, the next time we meet we can look more deeply at how both the facts and our opinions affect our reading.

. . . Good work today!

ASSESS AND PLAN

Did students confuse facts and opinions?

Sometimes readers' opinions, emotions, and reactions drown out the information they encounter as they read. In this session, we want to help kids realize how easy it is for our opinions to color the facts. If some kids seem to be confusing facts and opinions, consider conferring individually to help them record and code facts and opinions on Post-its. In the next session, we will help students consider what they have recorded and revise their opinions to reflect new information from the text.

Tie Your Opinions to Text Evidence

This session builds on the previous one. Students reconsider the information they have examined, rethink misconceptions, and revise their opinions to reflect new evidence and information from the text.

Companion to . . .

The Comprehension Toolkit
Lesson 25: Reread and Rethink

TEXT MATTERS

We continue exploring the text we used in the previous session.

CONSIDERATIONS FOR PLANNING

In the previous session, we invited students to record their thinking on Post-its and code facts and opinions. In this session, we offer them the opportunity to analyze their thinking and see how it changes when they are confronted with new information. The evolution of thought is at the heart of this session, and we want to scaffold kids into the awareness of how their thoughts and opinions sharpen when they recognize how their own opinions intersect with and change through reading.

Students will need their texts with Post-its from the previous session.

Students will need individual *Facts/Opinions/Changes in Thinking* charts.

SESSION GOAL

We want students to:
- revise thinking and opinions in the face of new evidence and information.

Build Background, Word and Concept Knowledge

TEACHING MOVES

- **Remind kids what they did** in the previous session. In this session, we build on the previous session and have kids analyze their opinions and the facts presented in the text.

- **Tell students they will reread** the text and their notes and see how their thinking changed. This session offers the opportunity to honor the reader's opinions but tempered and changed by the author's information.

TEACHING LANGUAGE

. . . Remember we talked when we last met about how we consider our own opinions and the facts presented by the author in a text.

. . . As readers, we want to engage with texts and have opinions. But when we read, we also open the door to having our ideas transformed and changed as we learn new information.

. . . We will get an opportunity to do that today as we reread and reconsider the text and our notes.

Teach /Model

- **Have kids review their Post-its** and share what they notice.

- **Introduce the chart.** Using the *Facts/Opinions/Changes in Thinking* form, we support students in increasing their awareness of how thinking and understanding evolve. You can find this form on page 64 in *The Comprehension Toolkit* Strategy Book 6: *Summarize and Synthesize*, or have kids create their own charts.

- **Model how to use the chart.** Read through your Post-its and record the facts, your opinions, and changes in your thinking. Show how you connect your opinions and the facts with arrows.

. . . Today we will take another look at the text and reconsider how we tracked our thinking on Post-its. It will be exciting to see how our opinions are influenced and changed by the facts the author presents.

. . . Turn and talk about the Post-its you wrote and coded during your reading.

. . . What do you notice?

. . . I have a chart I want to share with you.

Facts	Opinions	Changes in Thinking

. . . I'll show you how this works using my own Post-its. (Model reading through your Post-its and recording on the chart.) Here's a fact I jotted when we last met. I will record it on the chart in the *Facts* column.

. . . Here's a place where I had an opinion. I really feel strongly about . . . . As I read on, I realize my thinking changed from . . . to . . . . My thinking changed because I learned additional information, thought about it, and now I think . . . . I'll record that change in my thinking on the chart. And I'll show how I connected my opinion and the information with an arrow.

Guide/Support Practice

TEACHING MOVES

- **Have students do the same**—record the facts, their opinions, and their changes in thinking on the chart.

- **As kids read and record,** move among them to listen in and offer support as needed.

TEACHING LANGUAGE

. . . Now you reread and record on your own chart. We'll compare when you've had a chance to do that.

. . . I will be around to help you.

Wrap Up

TEACHING MOVES

- **Ask students to share** their thinking and how it evolved as they learned more information. For many students, this will be their first experience in analyzing thinking in this way. This paves the way for readers to become more critical and realize that reading can change thinking!

TEACHING LANGUAGE

. . . Who wants to share how your thinking changed as you considered your opinions and the facts that you read?

. . . Did anyone read something in the text that reinforced your own thinking? (Build on students' responses. Either situation may occur. Students may share how their ideas were changed or confirmed by information in the text.)

. . . Some of you may have some lingering questions that didn't get answered in the text. Those are important to pursue in further reading.

. . . Excellent work today!

Assess and Plan

Were students able to use the author's facts and their own opinions to analyze and identify changes in their own thinking?

Students will likely need more opportunities to engage in this kind of close reading and analysis. Consider offering students additional practice using the chart as they read other short texts about current topics from newspapers and periodicals, such as *Time for Kids*.

> *One place comprehended can make us understand other places better.*
> (Eudora Welty,
> *The Eye of the Story*)

Companion to . . .

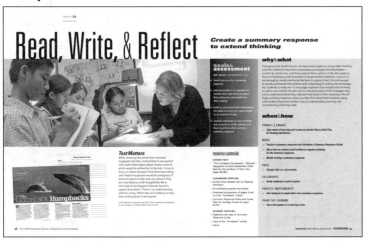

The Comprehension Toolkit
Lesson 26: Read, Write, and Reflect

Learn to Write a Summary

In *The Comprehension Toolkit* Lesson 26, students learn how to write a summary response. They use a *Summary Response Guide* to organize their thinking and then create a summary response for a read-aloud article. The four companion sessions for Lesson 26 offer students more support and scaffolding for learning to write a summary response. In this first session, they work with the teacher to create a standard summary.

Text Matters

We want to select a text that will bring students' curiosity to the surface, engaging them in reading and summarizing.

A short article that focuses on a current topic and has headings works well. "The Greenhouse Effect" in the *Source Book of Short Text*, "Shark!" in *Toolkit Texts: Grades 4–5*, and "Riding the Rails" and "Slithering Snakes" in *Toolkit Texts: Grades 2–3* have headings that will help kids organize summaries.

Session Goal

We want students to:
- learn how to write a summary.

Considerations for Planning

Summarizing has been described as the art of deletion. Even proficient readers sometimes struggle with how to abridge the author's message and capture the essence of a text.

This intervention is divided into four sessions to scaffold the summarizing process. Students will progress from writing a standard summary to merging their own thinking with the content and writing a summary response.

Selecting a section or two of text to summarize works best because of the short session timeframe. Kids can summarize another section in the following session.

Build Background, Word and Concept Knowledge

- Invite students to **review how they have grown** as readers of nonfiction. (Throughout *The Comprehension Toolkit* lessons and companion sessions, we focus on helping kids manage texts brimming with information. Using Post-its and note-taking forms, we show them how to read with consideration for what they bring as background knowledge and how they merge their thinking with information in the text. The result is enhanced understanding and the creation of richer schema as kids combine what they bring to the text with what they learn from it, and frequently modify their own thinking.)

- Explain that over the next four sessions they will **learn to write two kinds of summaries:** first a *standard summary* and then a *summary response*.

- A *standard summary* is a written summary that deletes interesting but unimportant details and redundant information and includes the gist of the text information and/or the author's message. Readers use subheads, text structure, and signal words to help them synthesize the important ideas in the text.

- A *summary response* briefly summarizes the important information and content, but it also includes the reader's thinking, responses, and reactions to the content.

. . . As we have studied nonfiction, we've learned so much about how we understand and learn from it. Turn and talk about some of the important things you know. (Help students name some of the ways in which they have grown as readers.)

. . . Right! You've learned some important ways to manage texts: using Post-it notes, charting, using note-taking strategies. You've also learned to take advantage of the ways authors organize text and provide either "right there" information or clues that lead readers to infer.

. . . Over our next four meetings, we will learn something else that is really important: how to write summaries. We'll learn two ways of writing summaries, and both will be helpful to you.

. . . The first kind of summary is a *standard summary*—one where we capture the author's key ideas. The second is a *summary response*. In that kind of summary, we go beyond merely summarizing the content, and we add our own thinking to the summary.

. . . Knowing how to write both types of summaries will be very helpful as you go through school.

. . . Today we will learn to write the first kind: the standard summary.

Teach/Model

TEACHING MOVES

■ **Preview the text together.** Discuss any unfamiliar vocabulary.

■ **Model the writing of a standard summary.** Show kids how to use what they've learned in previous sessions. By thinking aloud and naming how you use the text structure, text features, and author's signal words to help you record important ideas and then write a summary, you offer kids procedural knowledge they'll use to write their own summary in the next session.

■ **Summarize just a section or two.** Kids can summarize another section in the following session.

TEACHING LANGUAGE

. . . Let's preview the article together. Turn and talk about what you are thinking about the text and your own background knowledge.

. . . Good work! I love that you used the way the author organized the text to help you.

. . . Watch as I begin to read, using Post-its to record key ideas. (Read a section and think aloud as you note important information on Post-its. Ask kids to turn and talk about what they notice.)

. . . Now I'll pull off my Post-its to help me write my summary. I will lay them out, and just as we have done before, let's think about the importance of each idea.

. . . First let's delete the ideas that seem less important or redundant. Here are some details that are not important enough to include in our summary. And here are two Post-its that say almost the same thing. This is a signal that the idea is important, but I don't need to keep both!

. . . Let's see if I can combine any ideas. Yes, let's combine the information here . . . and here.

. . . Now I will arrange my remaining Post-its to write a summary. (Think aloud as you compose.)

. . . Turn and talk about what you noticed me doing.

. . . I could rearrange my Post-its and write a summary that's a bit different. Let's talk about some options, so you'll see there is not just one "right way" to write a summary. (Briefly discuss.)

Guide/Support Practice

▪ Ask kids to scan back through the text and **check the summary.**

. . . Scan back through the text. Does our summary make sense? Does it capture the most important ideas—the gist? Were we careful not to tell too much?

. . . Turn and talk. Then we'll share our thinking.

Wrap Up

▪ Ask students to review the process used to write the summary. **Record the steps on an anchor chart.**

▪ **Attach the summary** you wrote as a model.

. . . Very good thinking! Now let's make an anchor chart to capture the process we used to write the summary.

. . . I'll attach our summary as a model.

How to Write a Standard Summary
- Read the text and use Post-its to record important information.
- Take the Post-its and decide which information and ideas are most important.
- Look for information that says the same thing or could be combined.
- Organize the Post-its and write the summary.
- When you finish, ask, "Does my summary have all the most important information in the text? Did I keep it short and not tell too much?" To check, scan the text to be sure.

Standard Summary for _____

(attach your own example)

ASSESS AND PLAN

Did students seem confident evaluating the summary and listing the steps?

If kids don't seem confident, consider writing another model together with another section of the text before kids write their own summaries. However, you will review the process in the next session.

Write Your Own Summary

This session builds on the previous one. Students use what they have learned to write their own standard summary of an article.

Companion to . . .

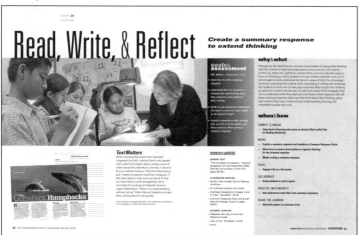

The Comprehension Toolkit
Lesson 26: Read, Write, and Reflect

Session Goal

We want students to:

■ write a standard summary.

Text Matters

Continue with the text from the previous session. If you finished that text with students, you may want to select another short, accessible text for kids to summarize. Suggestions for good text choices are offered in Text Matters in the previous session.

Considerations for Planning

In this second session, we review the procedures we modeled in the previous session so that students recall the model we provided. Then we invite them to read another piece of text and write their own standard summaries.

Have on hand the *How to Write a Standard Summary* anchor chart from the previous session.

Students will need Post-its.

Build Background, Word and Concept Knowledge

- **Review what a standard summary is.** Then review the process of writing one, using the anchor chart prepared in the previous session.

- **Listen for any confusion** about the process of summarizing and clarify if any exists. We want to set students up for success so they feel confident as they read and then write their summary.

. . . Who can remind us what a *standard summary* is? Right! It is one in which we summarize the author's most important ideas.

. . . Let's look back at the anchor chart we made. Turn and talk about what we did.

How to Write a Standard Summary

- Read the text and use Post-its to record important information.
- Take the Post-its and decide which information and ideas are most important.
- Look for information that says the same thing or could be combined.
- Organize the Post-its and write the summary.
- When you finish, ask, "Does my summary have all the most important information in the text? Did I keep it short and not tell too much?" To check, scan the text to be sure.

Standard Summary for _____

(attach your own example)

. . . Let's reconstruct what we did. Someone get us started. First, we . . .

. . . Today you'll read a text and write your own summary. What we have done is rehearse! You know how actors rehearse a play? Readers sometimes do something similar. They rehearse all the things they will do to perform a reading task!

Teach/Model

TEACHING MOVES

- **If kids will be reading a new article,** invite them to scan the article and share background knowledge before they begin to read and write Post-its.

- Encourage students to **refer to the anchor chart** as they proceed.

- You may want to **read and record a few Post-its** with kids to review that process before proceeding to the guided practice.

TEACHING LANGUAGE

. . . (If you are using a new text, preview it with kids.) Here's a great article for you to read. Scan it quickly. Turn and talk about what you notice *and* about your own background knowledge.

. . . We just reviewed—and rehearsed!—what we do as a reader and as a writer when we write a summary. You can refer to our anchor chart as you read and write your summary today.

. . . Now you're ready to read the article and write the important information on Post-its. (Consider beginning to read with students and writing one or two Post-its as models.)

Guide/Support Practice

TEACHING MOVES

- **Have students begin writing.** Give kids paper and remind them of the steps they will use to create their summaries.

- As kids read and write, move among them and **notice what they are writing on Post-its.** Confer with students who are recording small details rather than important information.

TEACHING LANGUAGE

. . . I will give everyone a blank piece of paper. You can write your summary on it. Then we can look at all our summaries.

. . . Remember, once you have finished reading and recording, take your Post-its and look them over. Make sure they sound like you—not the text!

. . . Look for ideas that are the same or can be combined.

. . . Then organize your Post-its. Put them in the order in which you'll write them up in your summary.

. . . Once you have your Post-its organized in a way that makes sense to you, you can use them to write your summary.

. . . I will be around to help you.

Wrap Up

TEACHING MOVES	TEACHING LANGUAGE

TEACHING MOVES

- Ask students to **share their summaries.**

- Have kids **summarize the process** they used.

TEACHING LANGUAGE

. . . I see you have finished your reading and have written your summary! Let's share them. (Have each student lay his or her summary on the table or floor.)

. . . Let's have each of you *summarize* what you did to write your summary! Now remember, this kind of summary is short!

ASSESS AND PLAN

Were students able to describe what they did to write their summaries?

As students learn new repertoires, it is helpful for them to use language as a tool for reviewing and remembering the performance. If students struggle with describing their actions, scaffold them in reviewing what they did. Consider individual conferences to further refine their understanding.

Did the summaries capture only the key information and ideas from the text?

Consider the qualitative aspects of each summary. If summaries lack the attributes of a quality standard summary, more models may be necessary. Keep in mind that learners often need to "consume" and "critique" many examples before becoming proficient!

> *There is no question that writing about reading aids comprehension and encourages readers to monitor their own reading strategies.*
> (Routman, 2005)

Companion to . . .

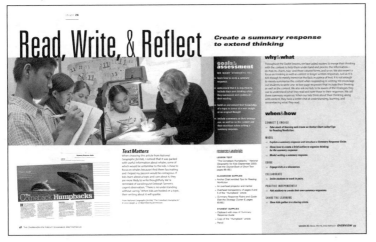

The Comprehension Toolkit
Lesson 26: Read, Write, and Reflect

Learn to Write a Summary Response

This session builds on the previous one. Using the *Summary Response Guide* planning tool, the teacher shows students how to extend thinking and write a summary response for the text they used in the previous session.

TEXT MATTERS

Continue to use the text used in the previous session. Using the same text will free kids' thinking energy to learn the process of writing a summary response.

CONSIDERATIONS FOR PLANNING

In this session, we build on the previous two. We help students transition to writing a summary response, which includes responding to the content and offers kids an opportunity to include their own thinking. The summary response is a good way to familiarize kids with the essay since it invites them to share their responses, reactions, opinions, and changes in thinking.

Have on hand the *How to Write a Standard Summary* anchor chart from the previous session.

You will need the summary you wrote in a previous session.

Students will need their summaries from the previous session.

Students will need individual copies of the *Summary Response Guide* from *The Comprehension Toolkit* Strategy Book 6: *Summarize and Synthesize*, page 66, or at the back of this book.

SESSION GOALS

We want students to:

- learn how to write a summary response.
- understand that it is important to include their own thinking when they summarize and synthesize their reading.
- build on and extend their knowledge of a topic to arrive at a new insight or an original thought.

Build Background, Word and Concept Knowledge

- **Review the standard summary.**

- **Explain what a *summary response* is.** A summary response differs from a standard summary in that it not only summarizes the important information and ideas from the text, but also includes the reader's own thinking, responses, and reactions to the content.

. . . We have been talking about standard summaries. Who can tell us what a standard summary is?

. . . Now we'll learn about a summary response. Think about those two words: *summary* and *response*.

. . . In a summary response, we do as we have been doing; we write a summary. But, we also merge our own thinking with the content. A standard summary is brief—if the summary is longer than what we read, it isn't a summary! In a summary response, we write more because we include our own responses and reactions to the content.

Teach/Model

- Ask kids to **review the standard summaries** they wrote in the previous session.

- **Introduce the *Summary Response Guide.*** Give students a copy to take notes on as you demonstrate. A form you can copy is provided in *The Comprehension Toolkit* Strategy Book 6: *Summarize and Synthesize*, page 66, or at the back of this book.

- **Model the process** of completing the *Summary Response Guide* and writing your own summary response. The purpose we set for ourselves as readers influences the way we read. When we make it transparent to students that our purpose in reading or rereading has shifted, it helps them proceed strategically and increases their potential for success.

- **Have students take notes** on their copies as you model how to use the *Summary Response Guide.*

. . . Let's quickly look over the summaries we wrote last time. . . . They capture just the important information and ideas, right? Here's the one I wrote.

. . . Today we will use a planning tool called the *Summary Response Guide* to help us take our standard summaries and turn them into summary responses. (Give kids the form.)

. . . I'm going to reread the text. This time I will use Post-its to record my responses and my thinking as I read. (Demonstrate how you reread with this different purpose.)

. . . Turn and talk about what you notice I am doing.

. . . Now I am going to use the *Summary Response Guide.* Take notes on your copy as I demonstrate. I'm going to write the key ideas from my standard summary in the area labeled *CONTENT.* (Think aloud for kids as you write.)

. . . Remember that as I reread, I wrote Post-its capturing my responses and reactions. I was merging my thinking with the information I was reading. Now I'll take my Post-its off the text and lay them out. Watch as I record these ideas on my form in the area labeled *MERGED THINKING.*

. . . As I do this, I realize I am still learning how connecting my own background knowledge helps me read much better. I'll record that in the area labeled *STRATEGY USE.*

. . . Now I will use my notes on the form to help me as I write my summary response. (Model writing your summary response so that students hear and see your composing process. Invite kids to turn and talk as you write.)

Guide/Support Practice

TEACHING MOVES

■ **Create another anchor chart** to show the process for writing a summary response. Build on the steps for a standard summary and add the new steps for a summary response.

TEACHING LANGUAGE

. . . Let's create another anchor chart to show how we write a summary response.

. . . Here's the anchor chart we created before. (Show the anchor chart for *How to Write a Standard Summary*.) Turn and talk about what we might need to add.

. . . Good thinking! Let's capture that on our new chart.

How to Write a Summary Response

- Read the text and use Post-its to record important information.
- Take the Post-its and decide which information and ideas are most important.
- Look for information that says the same thing or could be combined.
- Reread the text and use Post-its to record personal responses, reactions, and merged thinking.
- Review all the Post-its and write a summary response that includes your own responses and a comment about a strategy that helped you understand.

Summary Response for _____

(attach your own example)

Wrap Up

TEACHING MOVES

- Ask kids what they noticed about **how a summary response differs** from a standard summary.

- Invite students to **share their thinking** about the content.

TEACHING LANGUAGE

. . . Who can quickly tell us how a summary response differs from a standard summary?

. . . What are you thinking about the content of this text? Turn and talk.

. . . Good thinking! Now keep all that in mind because you'll have a chance to write your own summary response when we meet again.

ASSESS AND PLAN

Did students note the similarities and differences between the two types of summaries?

The standard summary is challenging for some students. Adding additional components increases the complexity of the task. If you note confusion, consider "sharing the pen" with students to coauthor a summary response before proceeding to the next session.

Through our patterns of behavior, thinking, and interaction, we show what we are made of as thinkers and learners. . . . This is the kind of long-term vision we need for education: to be shapers of students' intellectual character. (Ritchhart, 2002)

Companion to . . .

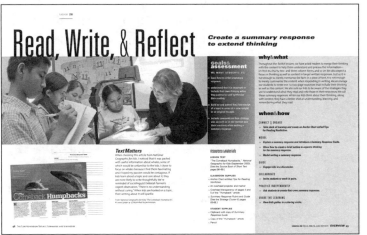

The Comprehension Toolkit
Lesson 26: Read, Write, and Reflect

SESSION GOALS

We want students to:

- learn how to write a summary response.

- understand that it is important to include their own thinking when they summarize and synthesize their reading.

- build on and extend their knowledge of a topic to arrive at a new insight or an original thought.

- include comments on their strategy use, as well as on the content and their reactions when writing a summary response.

Write Your Own Summary Response

This session builds on the previous one. Students review the process they learned in the previous session and write their own summary response of the article.

TEXT MATTERS

We continue to use the same text used in the previous session.

CONSIDERATIONS FOR PLANNING

In this final session, we build on the previous three sessions and on the work we have done throughout our comprehension study. As students transition to the summary response, we help support the process by coaching and scaffolding as needed.

Have on hand the *How to Write a Summary Response* anchor chart from the previous session.

Students will need their standard summaries from Session 26b, Post-its, and new copies of the *Summary Response Guide*.

Build Background, Word and Concept Knowledge

- Invite kids to **review the two types of summaries.**

- Have students read over and **discuss the anchor chart** for writing a summary response.

. . . Today you will get the chance to write your own summary response!

. . . Turn and talk about what you know about the two types of summaries and the process for writing each.

. . . Take a look at our anchor chart, *How to Write a Summary Response.* Turn and talk about what you will do. This is a chance to rehearse before you write!

How to Write a Summary Response

- Read the text and use Post-its to record important information.
- Take the Post-its and decide which information and ideas are most important.
- Look for information that says the same thing or could be combined.
- Reread the text and use Post-its to record personal responses, reactions, and merged thinking.
- Review all the Post-its and write a summary response that includes your own responses and a comment about a strategy that helped you understand.

Summary Response for _____

(attach your own example)

Teach/Model

<table>
<tr><td>TEACHING MOVES</td><td>TEACHING LANGUAGE</td></tr>
</table>

TEACHING MOVES

- **Give students a new copy** of the *Summary Response Guide* introduced in the previous session.

- Have students review their standard summaries and **fill in the first section** of the *Summary Response Guide*.

- **Have students reread the text,** recording their personal responses and merged thinking on Post-its. When they finish, invite them to turn and talk.

- As students **proceed through the *Summary Response Guide*,** encourage them to turn and talk about each section. Be sure they understand what they are to do.

TEACHING LANGUAGE

. . . I'm giving you each a new copy of our *Summary Response Guide*.

. . . Look over the standard summary you wrote. Write the key ideas on the *Summary Response Guide* in the first section, *CONTENT.*

. . . Now reread the text. This time, use Post-its to record your responses and thinking as you read. Remember how I did that?

. . . Now that you've finished reading and writing Post-its, turn and talk about your personal responses and merged thinking.

. . . Look over your Post-its and record your ideas in the area labeled *MERGED THINKING.*

. . . Turn and talk about strategies you used that helped you when you read. Jot those in the area labeled *STRATEGY USE.*

. . . Now you have good notes on the form to help you as you write your summary response.

. . . What questions do you have?

Guide/Support Practice

- **Have students write** their summary responses. They may need to talk before they write. Talk is often an important way to rehearse before writing.

- **If you see kids struggling** to write, invite them to talk. Provide more support for their writing by jotting down what they say on a Post-it. In this way, we leave tracks of their own words as a scaffold for writing.

. . . Now it's your turn to write a summary response.

. . . We will work together on this. You may want to do some talking as you are preparing to write.

. . . When you start to write, I will be around to work with each of you.

Wrap Up

- **Have kids share their summaries.**

. . . Today you wrote a different kind of summary. I can tell you enjoyed writing these!

. . . I know some of you would like to share. First turn and share with a partner. Then we can share in our group.

. . . Super work! I can tell that these summaries helped you understand the content much better.

ASSESS AND PLAN

Were students able to write the summary response with relative ease? If not, what parts were challenging?

When students experience difficulty, we often reteach a whole lesson. Yet by listening to students talk about their process, we can frequently pinpoint where their understanding or process broke down. It is at that point that we need to coach and support. Talk with any student who experienced difficulty. Identify the point at which the performance "wobbled" and coach from that point.

Summarize and Synthesize

After this unit, you want to know that students are able to synthesize the information and come up with the big ideas as they read, so your conference should help the student sift through the details to get the gist of a piece as he or she reads.

1. **Invite the student to choose a passage and tell what the whole book or article is about.**
   - Choose a part of your text and read it to me.
   - What is the big idea of your book or article?

2. **Ask the student to paraphrase what she or he just read.**
   - Put the information into your own words and share the gist of the piece you read.

3. **Focus on the student's ability to synthesize, draw conclusions, and come up with the big ideas in the text.**
   - Share a Post-it or some margin notes that show that you have been stopping and responding to the information as you read, synthesizing as you go.
   - Show a place where you put together some facts to come up with a bigger idea in the text.
   - Share some details that are interesting but may not be that important to understanding the bigger ideas in the text.

4. **Discuss standard summaries and summary responses.**
   Note: For the most meaningful assessment, evaluate the summaries the student created in class.
   - What are some of the ideas you would include if you were writing a summary of this piece?
   - Tell me about the standard summary and summary response you wrote in class.

Reading Conference Recording Form: Summarize and Synthesize	
Name _____ Date _____	
Book title _____	
GOAL	**EVIDENCE**
The student . . .	This student . . .
1. Understands the text • Tells about the passage he or she read • Talks about the book's or article's big ideas	
2. Puts information into his or her own words and paraphrases the text • Retells facts from the text in her or his own words (paraphrases) • Includes important information that relates to the key ideas	
3. Synthesizes facts and draws conclusions to come up with the bigger ideas and issues • Separates the ancillary details from the bigger ideas to get the gist	
4. Creates a standard summary and a summary response • The summary contains the most important information. • Important ideas are organized logically. • The summary response includes personal thinking about the big ideas in the summary.	Note: For the most meaningful assessment, evaluate the summaries the student created in class.

©2010 by Stephanie Harvey, Anne Goudvis, and Judy Wallis. From *Comprehension Intervention: Small-Group Lessons for The Comprehension Toolkit.* Portsmouth, NH: Heinemann. This page may be copied for classroom use only.

Conference Recording Form for "Summarize and Synthesize," located in "Resources" section.

Follow-Ups

If the student has difficulty with any of the primary goals in this unit, prompts like the following may be helpful during independent work in subsequent units.

- Did you remember to stop and think frequently as you were reading?
- Did you put the information into your own words?
- What do you think are some of the big ideas here?
- Did you use the facts to come up with some of the bigger ideas here?
- Did any new ideas pop into your head as you were reading?
- Did you change your mind about anything as you read?
- How did your thinking change as you read?

Language students may use
to demonstrate that they are summarizing and synthesizing the information

- The big idea here is . . .
- To sum up . . .
- A new idea I had here was . . .
- The gist of this piece was . . .
- I used to think . . . , but now I think . . .
- I never realized . . .

Resources

Reading Conference Recording Forms

Monitor Comprehension

Activate and Connect

Ask Questions

Infer Meaning

Determine Importance

Summarize and Synthesize

Summary Response Guide

Reading Conference Recording Form: Monitor Comprehension

Name _____ Date _____

Book title _____

GOAL	EVIDENCE
The student . . .	**This student . . .**
1. Understands the text • Tells what the book is about and talks about what she or he was thinking while reading	
2. Is aware of his or her own monitoring strategies • Responds to text while reading, for example, wondering about content, relating it to something he or she knows, noting when she or he doesn't understand • Jots down thoughts and reactions to reading	
3. Knows fix-up strategies for regaining meaning • Explains what to do when she or he doesn't understand part of the text	

Reading Conference Recording Form: Activate and Connect

Name _____ Date _____

Book title _____

GOAL	EVIDENCE
The student . . .	**This student . . .**
1. Understands the text • Tells what the book is about and what he or she learned by reading it	
2. Notices and uses text and visual features • Identifies text and visual features and talks about the information he or she learned from them • Explains the purpose of features	Note: Use only if the student is reading nonfiction with visual/text features.
3. Uses background knowledge to understand new information • Notices and reacts when the text confirms something she or he already knew • Uses language that signals new learning	
4. Identifies inaccurate prior knowledge and changes thinking based on new information • Tells how new information cleared up a misconception	

Reading Conference Recording Form: Ask Questions

Name _____ Date _____

Book title _____

GOAL	EVIDENCE
The student . . .	**This student . . .**
1. Understands and questions the text • Tells what the text is about and asks questions about it	
2. Asks questions and tries to answer them • Stops and asks a question to clarify meaning, to clear up confusion, or to express curiosity • Notices when his or her questions are answered • Recognizes that not all questions are answered when reading	
3. Reads with a question in mind and uses a variety of strategies to answer the question • Skims and scans to find answers • Reads on • Talks about it	

Reading Conference Recording Form: Infer Meaning

Name _____ Date _____

Book title _____

GOAL	EVIDENCE
The student . . .	**This student . . .**
1. Understands the text • Tells what the book is about and talks about what he or she was thinking while reading	
2. Is aware of his or her own visualizing and inferring strategies • Describes and explains inferences and mental images • Combines text clues with background knowledge to understand a difficult part • (If reading nonfiction with features) Infers information from features	
3. Infers to answer questions • Asks a question and makes inferences to answer it	
4. Infers and visualizes to surface big ideas and themes • Uses inferring and visualizing to surface big ideas and themes • Supports big ideas and themes with text evidence	

Reading Conference Recording Form: Determine Importance

Name _____ Date _____

Book title _____

GOAL	EVIDENCE
The student . . .	**This student . . .**
1. Understands the text • Tells what the book is about and what she or he learned by reading it	
2. Describes how he or she sifts interesting details from important information • Explains how facts, questions, and responses supported learning new information • Tells how note-taking scaffolds, coding the text, and margin notes help sort and sift information	
3. Distinguishes between the reader's thinking and the author's thinking • Notes the difference between what he or she wants to remember and what the author thinks is important • Discerns the difference between her or his own perspective and the author's perspective or opinions	

Reading Conference Recording Form: Summarize and Synthesize

Name _____   Date _____

Book title _____

GOAL	EVIDENCE
The student . . .	**This student . . .**
1. Understands the text • Tells about the passage he or she read • Talks about the book's or article's big ideas	
2. Puts information into his or her own words and paraphrases the text • Retells facts from the text in her or his own words (paraphrases) • Includes important information that relates to the key ideas	
3. Synthesizes facts and draws conclusions to come up with the bigger ideas and issues • Separates the ancillary details from the bigger ideas to get the gist	
4. Creates a standard summary and a summary response • The summary contains the most important information. • Important ideas are organized logically. • The summary response includes personal thinking about the big ideas in the summary.	Note: For the most meaningful assessment, evaluate the summaries the student created in class.

Name _____ Date _____

Summary Response Guide
Elements to use in a Summary Response:

CONTENT
Important information and ideas from the reading

_____
_____
_____
_____
_____
_____
_____

MERGED THINKING
My thinking about the information and ideas

_____
_____
_____
_____
_____
_____
_____
_____

STRATEGY USE
How a strategy helped me understand the information and ideas

_____
_____
_____
_____
_____
_____
_____
_____